STAY WITH WRITING

STAY WITH WRITING

Practices for Sustaining the Writer's Work and Life

Cindy Shearer

BLOOMSBURY ACADEMIC
LONDON • NEW YORK • OXFORD • NEW DELHI • SYDNEY

BLOOMSBURY ACADEMIC
Bloomsbury Publishing Plc, 50 Bedford Square, London, WC1B 3DP, UK
Bloomsbury Publishing Inc, 1359 Broadway, New York, NY 10018, USA
Bloomsbury Publishing Ireland, 29 Earlsfort Terrace, Dublin 2, D02 AY28, Ireland

BLOOMSBURY, BLOOMSBURY ACADEMIC and the Diana logo are
trademarks of Bloomsbury Publishing Plc

First published in Great Britain 2026

A catalogue record for this book is available from the British Library.

A catalog record for this book is available from the Library of Congress.

ISBN: HB: 978-1-3504-5544-3
         PB: 978-1-3504-5545-0
         ePDF: 978-1-3504-5546-7
         eBook: 978-1-3504-5547-4

Typeset by RefineCatch Limited, Bungay, Suffolk
Printed and bound in Great Britain

For product safety related questions contact
productsafety@bloomsbury.com.

To find out more about our authors and books visit
www.bloomsbury.com and sign up for our newsletters.

For Jason

CONTENTS

FIGURES

AUTHOR BIOGRAPHY

Cindy Shearer is Professor and Program Chair for the MFA in Interdisciplinary Arts and Writing, California Institute of Integral Studies (CIIS), San Francisco, CA. With Debashish Banerji, she co-designed and co-leads the Creative Dissertation Pathway within the PhD in East-West Psychology at CIIS. A writer, text/image artist, and curator, she recently presented "Traces of Space and Time: Built and Designed Places and Visual Writing/Artmaking," at the AMPS, Learning, Life, Work Conference, 2024, which she co-chaired. Her art practice and research interests include text/image artwork, creative inquiry, and art practice as research.

ACKNOWLEDGMENTS

Many thanks to Lucy Brown for inviting me to write this book; thank you for your support and generosity. Thank you to Aanchal Vij for your kind editorial guidance.

Thank you to Julie and Theresa for supporting me and our degree programs every day—and for all the ways you've supported me while writing this book. Many thanks to Kris for support for many years. Thank you, Nupu, for reading this work in draft, the great conversations—and the care you have given me and this book.

Many thanks to Nelson Melgar for the photos of *Chilton House*, *Puzzle*, *This Is My Mother's Grave*, *Lost-proof*, and *Portrait: The Man*, Glen Graves for the photo of *Haiku Box*, and Bob Stender for photos of *Green Tara: Where Are you?* and *Ten Not-So-Tangible Tools for Writers Toolbox*.

Thank you and love to Jason and Marina. Thank you to my brother for being part of Chapter 2.

Portions of Chapter 3: Stay With It were originally published in "The Art of Being: Why the Inter-arts Matter for Writers," *Exploring Creative Writing: Voices from the Great Writing International Creative Writing Conference*, CSP Publishers, 2016. Published here with the permission of Cambridge Scholars Publishing. Many thanks as well to Graeme Harper.

Many thanks to Michael Garbutt and Nico Roenpagel for the chance to explore some early thoughts on offering and artmaking, image as seeing, and my parents' stories in "The Art of Image: Seeing the Way Home," in M. Garbutt & N. Roenpagel (Eds) & A. Rourke and V. Rees (Series Curators), *The Mindful Eye: Contemplative Pedagogies in Visual Arts Education*. Transformative Pedagogies in The Visual Domain: Book No. 3. Champaign, IL: Common Ground Research Networks, 2018. Thanks for supporting me in drawing from it for this book.

Thank you also to Kertsin Hof, Medical School Hamburg, for many years of interest and support for writing as art—and for allowing me to reflect on art as poetic offering in Hof, Kerstin (ed.)"Offerings: A Poetic Approach to Text and Image," *Dreierlei Mut. Collagen zur Relevanz von*

Poesie, Literatur & Schreiben in Gesellschaft & Gesundheit, Berlin: Germany: HBP University Press, 2020. Thanks for supporting me in drawing from it for this book.

Portions of Chapter 1: Elliott, Found and Loss were originally published in *Mission at Tenth*, Volume 6, 2015, as "Beautiful Brevities: Image, Memory and the Art of Seeing." An earlier version of "Dementia Moment," included in Chapter 3: Stay With It, was published in *Mission at Tenth*, Volume 2, 2011.

Draft versions of "At Home," "Yellow Room," and "The Shoebox Sewing Box" were originally posted in my Work in Progress Series on www.cindyshearer.com

INTRODUCTION: START THERE, WHY NOT?

I started writing this book—very aware of my submission due date—and then I broke my shoulder, a totally random thing. I walk every morning—the same walk, same number of steps, same terrain. I don't vary the route much at all. I could probably do it in my sleep.

I stepped onto the usual dirt path that connects a San Rafael elementary school and a former district school, now a private school for children kindergarten to eighth grade. It does have some ruts, rocks, tufts of grass, uneven places, but, like me, parents, grandparents, caretakers, bicyclers, strollers, toddlers, dogs and dog walkers, safely navigate it each day, so the risk was less than minimal. For no reason, except it had been a good morning, I said to myself, "Things are working out," and then I smacked into the ground. I don't remember catching on something, but later I discovered a scrubby, uneven bit of grass near where I fell. Maybe my toe caught it. I feel a lot better saying my foot snagged on something than I have no idea what happened. I do remember I had maybe a second to throw my hands out and probably break my wrist or keep my arm close to my body and land on my shoulder. I was too much in free fall to decide; my shoulder struck against unforgiving ground. Later, the Physician's Assistant would refer to my crushed (not fractured) bone.

I couldn't figure out to how to get up; I was stuck on my right side. I couldn't use my right arm; it was cemented into my side. I tried to roll over, hoping I could push up from my left side, but no go. I needed help from my upper body I didn't have. Please don't try this: Instead, I lifted my left foot since it seemed the only part of my body that was mobile (actually, I mostly used the big toe) and dug it into the ground and pushed myself up. The next day and for weeks the toe and left side of my foot were swollen and horribly black and blue.

I couldn't take in what had happened. I was a mess—dirt on my clothes, leaves in my hair—but my mind told me it was okay, I was fine, maybe nothing much really happened. I was deep in magical thinking, sure I would just walk home and everything would be okay.

It took ten days to get the MRI that revealed why I couldn't move my arm. Four x-rays revealed no break, one MRI revealed a comminuted, nondisplaced fracture of the humeral head greater tuberosity, the aforementioned crushed bone. The orthopedist breezed in to say I would not need surgery (the good news) but that I must wear a sling and could not move the shoulder for six weeks (the exasperating news). He said six to nine months for full recovery, that once the bone healed, I would need physical therapy, first to work on range of motion and ultimately on strength.

This book became a very hard thing. I could barely function, struggling to get done what was needed for my teaching, administrative work—and my life—let alone write. Brushing my teeth, stepping into or out of the shower, turning the key in the lock of my front door, figuring out how to pull a blouse or a sweatshirt over my head and through a sleeve, putting on a bra or zipping up a jacket, even trying to cut my toast with my left hand, all were difficult and labor intensive because my right side was immobilized and I'm right-handed. I took for granted that I could lift my right arm so I could use it on the computer keyboard—until I couldn't. For the better part of two months, I could hardly move and that meant on this book as well.

I began to wonder—Did I have it in me to make progress, let alone, finish the book? Who was I kidding? Did I even have anything interesting, even relevant, to say?

My thinking grew tired, the small amounts of writing I did got tired, I was tired. As the shoulder got the tiniest bit better, I realized I needed to get away from all the ways I felt overwhelmed and find a way to write. I needed to re-build my writing mobility and strength, same as I would for my shoulder. Just make something, write one thing instead of thinking about writing a book—maybe I'd start there. I was creating a book about taking on failure and building a sustainable writer's life—and I couldn't get a damn thing done.

I forgot and had to remind myself I had stories I wanted to tell, some I'd carried for more than forty years. Start there, why not? I first wrote stories about Elliott Coleman, an early writing mentor, one by one. Then, I told stories about why I quit writing and how I found a way back to it, and finally about the art and artists I've connected with who also sustain me and my writing. I followed a simple plan: See the story and write what I see. Be curious about each story and if or how each related to the others. I probed what I remembered, what I researched to augment my memory, what pieces I'd already written told me. I was trying to see what connected the stories, why that mattered. I kept that up as I wrote.

Fun fact: I watched Jimmy Fallon's *Classroom Instruments* concert with Sheryl Crow, and the pure play of it incited me to write. I started watching You Tube videos of pop music performances. More *Classroom Instruments* with Jimmy Fallon and others and *Tiny Desk* concerts on NPR were go-to listens as were other tracks arising from whatever rabbit-hole the algorithms suggested as it followed my listening history. I could tap play or cancel, a popular culture version of *be here now* but with dance steps and chances to singalong. Also, when it was time to perform, the performers showed up; no one said, I don't think I can do this today. They got a cue to start and they did. Watching was fun, a distraction from what was keeping me from writing. Weirdly, it gave me a way in.

I started putting an X through hours or days on my calendar to step out of my regular work life and into my writing. All I had to do was look at my schedule and see when I was writing. I made progress, not perfect progress—some days, like today, I have been working for hours, but I also took a break to go to the grocery store, eat lunch, catch up on tennis scores, and have an ice cream cone.

I have not had a pretty process, but I have done the work. I have reflected on what I recall and what I know—and what I needed to learn to write this book. I have scoured definitions, researched Chilton House, the Odd Fellows, narrative architecture, and many other things, searched Google maps, drafted text, made notes about books and artwork, reviewed my images and postcards, remembered as many details as I could —and stayed with it. I've been curious about my life and probed events that affected it. My choices as writer/artist have been in an ongoing dialogue with the choices in the rest of my life—and the realities that inform them—and I drafted the book.

I've relied on memoir and essay, bringing together, often blending, the two to try to show this. I've wanted you to see what and how I see, so you can choose what you want to take from what is shown. The origins of *memoir* and *essay* inspire how I've written each chapter and the relationship I hope the writing creates with you: I've attempted to share with you what (and why) I've recalled certain things (kept them in mind), while also weighing what to say and how to speak to you: *Memoire* refers to "something written to be kept in mind" and *essai* "an attempt" and *exagium* "a weighing." My hope is your reading is consequential (in good ways) and fun.

*   *   *

I recently had coffee with Kary, one of our MFA graduates. When I shared with her some choices I was making in writing this book, she said, well, just be inspiring, that is what you do well.

I feel very humbled by and appreciative of what she said. [Thank you.]

And—she got me thinking about what it means to inspire and the responsibility inherent in that.

I realized being inspiring can be a very good thing, but being inspired can be a fleeting experience. What I'd like to do is inspire you in ways you can tangibly carry forward, so you have something genuine that uplifts you but also that you can rely on again and again.

I often inspire myself on my morning walks when I am not breaking bones. I imagine what I might say in a scene or sentence and suddenly I am excited to write. Then I get home, and something distracts me and, whether it is minutes or hours before I get to write anything down, I can't reconnect with what was so great about what I had to say.

Or I immediately write it all down—and quickly I see the holes in or limits of the great prose in my head or that it is confusing or wrong (not brilliant!). It sounded so much better in my head than it does on the page.

The inspiration was good, motivating, but did it help me to stay with the process and make the work?

Maybe, instead, it's time to write and a song inspires me to get to work (see above). Or I connect with a memory, image, comment, quote, or poem that encourages me to get started or keep going—and I do. I'd like to help you feel that way, but more important to me, I hope as you read this book and, in particular, once you set it down and step into your work, that what I offer here provides support you can draw on, while also encouraging you to be curious about your choices and the directions of your work—my failures, losses, short-sightedness, indecision, joy, good decisions, learning, success, and all the beauty I've experienced is an ally you can count on and return to while you are deciding what works for you. That, like Alonzo King, who you'll meet in Chapter 3, I am saying keep going/stay with it—stay with it. And you do.

*   *   *

This book originated, in part, from a workshop I gave to the National Association of Writers in Education (NAWE) on failure, quitting, and trying again. I was also inspired [!] to probe Hisham Matar's statement that writing is a "magnificent failure" from the *New York Times* review of his book *My Friends*. I appreciate his view that writing/artmaking is always approximate, never perfect—and that awareness of that can even be motivating.

My experience is failure and loss permeate the making of creative work. Failure is everywhere in the process and always within what's produced. There is not being able to achieve what we want, not being good enough, not finding an audience or a publisher, not finishing or not getting a chance to complete the work (loss of funding or opportunity or time), others not liking the work or not needing it or changing what they want from it or not publishing it—I have failed in all these ways and many more.

In *Stay With Writing*, I focus more on loss—and what can be found—than failure. I've learned from loss—and what I've found in others and with others helps me sustain how I navigate failure. I want to show you how and why they can sustain you too.

A few things to guide your reading of this book—

- For me, creative writers are artists who use text to make art, so I use the words *writer* and *artist* interchangeably. When I say making art or something like that, I mean writing as well as other arts.

- *Reflection Journal*: Please have a notebook you can use while you read this book (or a place to type or record notes, if you prefer). I like notebooks/journals with blank pages (and heavier paper) but any notebook/sketchbook will work well. I am using one by Allan Weir at Native Northwest, with blank pages on the left and lined pages on the right. Bienfang makes a Notesketch Pad with blank space and lines on the same page. I hope you'll reflect on this question as you read: What do the stories and choices I share encourage you to consider and learn from yours?

- *Reflection Sections*. I provide exercises and items for you to reflect on in each chapter. I guide you in the making of your own resources—tools or cards—and maybe a few postcards (stay tuned for more on that). In the final chapter, I suggest how you can gather your insights/tools and use them to help you sustain and stay with your writing.

- *Resources and References*: In Resources (included in each chapter), I provide links to websites for artists I refer to, for definitions, or more about artwork, directions, events, information I've used creatively or informally often from a quick Internet search. If I quote a phrase or word or briefly provide information, I'm trying to further my inquiry or clarify, and it is not formally cited, but the links provided connect you to at least one resource I drew from. The Reference section provides bibliographic information for cited items.

Resources

"Sheryl Crow, Jimmy Fallon & The Roots Sing 'All I Wanna Do' (Classroom Instruments)." YouTube video, 3:29. Posted by The Tonight Show Starring Jimmy Fallon, Nov. 3, 2023. https://www.youtube.com/watch?v=FXHQGHEkj1s

Origins of *Essay* and *Memoir*: Essay: https://www.etymonline.com/search?q=essay and Memoir: https://www.etymonline.com/search?q=memoir

"Writing Is Doomed to Fail. That's Why Hisham Matar Loves It." *NY Times*, Jan 10, 2024. https://www.nytimes.com/2024/01/10/books/hisham-matar-my-friends.html?pvid–QdntZFlsrNvdMLrYTb-mVpc&smid=url-share.

1 ELLIOT, FOUND AND LOSS

I: Found—A Way to See

Seeing

In 1978, I sat by myself at a breakfast table at Plater College in Oxford. I was twenty-one, had left my home and relationships behind, to travel to England to work on a master's degree in creative writing at Antioch University's Centre for British Studies. I would spend the summer in Oxford and then a year in London.

So many things were new for me that summer—and that morning, the learning curve felt steep. I'd never been on an airplane before flying from Dayton, Ohio, via New York, to London. It seemed that, in honor of my inexperience, TWA sold out coach class, giving me the chance to buy a first-class seat for my flight to JFK. There, I was to take a charter flight with the rest of the students in my program to Gatwick but, when I arrived, there was an impromptu baggage handlers' strike. I waited (and waited) for my luggage. I didn't know not to do that—that I should go ahead and confirm my flight—and by the time I made my way to my gate, my overbooked flight to London was full. The cabin door was closed; the charter company had given away my seat. I got a food voucher and a hotel room for the night. Instead of Antioch shepherding my too-many suitcases, manual typewriter, and me from Gatwick to Oxford, I had to find the way on my own.

By the time I made it to Oxford, I was almost two days late and felt well out of sync—so it makes sense to me now that the first morning at breakfast, I was quietly eating alone. I can't really remember or I'm not sure why the elderly man who entered the breakfast room just as I was leaving so profoundly caught my eye. I tell myself it was the force of white in his presence—and his amazing bright, blue eyes. His skin was clear, almost translucent, like watery milk, and his hair and beard a soft, knitted white. He was six-feet-something tall and seemed to glow. The contrasting whites were thin and thick, vibrant and dense—and later I'd see all those things and more in his personality. I needed a friend, even one who was fifty years older than me. I hoped Elliott Coleman would become mine.

In the mid-1940s, Elliott founded and then directed the Writing Seminars at Johns Hopkins University, one of the first elite creative writing programs in the United States—and he had recently retired. He came to Oxford at the request of his friend and the Antioch writing program director, Michael Lynch. Naïve as I was, I still picked up the retirement was not entirely voluntary—and there were other concerns plaguing Elliott, particularly his health. He'd suffered a stroke, which hampered his ability to walk on his own, let alone take care of himself, and made it difficult for him to use his writing hand. That inability, or perhaps some unwillingness to retrain his hand, would lead to a writing technique that allowed him to create his last book and would become instrumental to me.

I came to Antioch and England to learn to write, really become a writer, and Elliott had his lifetime of wisdom to impart. I wanted him to be receptive to visits from me, so taking a cue from the lesson offered by my recent flying experience, I decided not to hesitate. I decided to buy my way into getting to know him. I heard Elliott liked chocolate—I discovered Cadbury bars. Then, I learned he liked roses—thank you, England, for so easily accommodating that. I was also told he loved Beefeater's Gin and crisp chardonnay, even though he wasn't supposed to drink alcohol anymore. To be safe, I brought a bottle of each and no longer needed to worry about being invited to visit. I had a standing invitation each day.

Seeing Into

Although I got to know Elliott more than forty-five years ago in Oxford, I carry a vivid image of him creating poems from his bed in a senior home in Chilton, England. At the end of the summer, when we, as students, made the move to London, Michael Lynch and Elliott found

Chilton House in Buckinghamshire, near Thame. Then, once a week, Michael, Stephanie, a former nun, also a student in the program, and I, were lucky enough to meet with him there. The weekly conferences were set up as a tutorial for Stephanie and me, but, in the end, we all shared work—and the great gift to me during that time was the chance to sit inside Elliott's writing process.

Between our visits, Elliott pondered his life, read as best he could (another consequence of his health), followed the news about the impending Pope (he was so excited about John Paul II), and wrote poetry. He was a great example that writers write, even if they can't write down what they write. Elliott wrote in his mind and preserved what he wrote in his memory. During the week, he would create a poem—word by word— embedding it in his brain, and when we arrived, he would dictate it—one of us recording what he said (he told us the line breaks and the breaths as well as the words) until the poem made it fully to paper. I was struck always by how deeply he listened to himself—how as he spoke the poem, it was as if he too was hearing it for the first time. Often, as soon as the poem was spoken, a plan for revising was stirring in his mind.

But the most important thing I learned from Elliott's writing process was how writing can be seeing—seeing in images. In *What It Is*, graphic memoirist and cartoonist, Lynda Barry writes, "What is an image? It's the pull toy that pulls you, takes you from one place to another" (2008, 122). I was lucky to be a witness to how Elliott created many of the poems for what would become his final collection, *Four Counties of Youth*, which I would publish, but his process of creating "Remembrance of Princeton," (1980, 14) showed me how the willingness to see in images benefits the writer. Each memory became an image that pulled him toward another until his seeing of each was full and complete.

Remembrances of Princeton
To Sister Miriam

Beautiful brevities: the small letters of
New Testament Greek and Dr. Einstein
eating an ice cream cone on Mercer Street

This poem started out long—a list of memories, which were really images, of a short time (a summer or a semester? I can't remember) Elliott spent in Princeton. *Image* has origins in Old French, "to form a mental picture of"—and that was what Elliott did. He visualized and then used words to "image" each moment. For me, it was as if there was a short film of his experience playing through his mind, and he captured a still to view on its own and see it in relationship to others. One after another they accumulated and finally contained his experience. Then, in the revision process, he would let them define his experience.

Once Elliott had a list, he began to whittle it down. He discovered that writing each image in his mind required him to really see it. When he looked closely, he realized that some images coincided with his felt sense (his image) of his experience, and others didn't. Really seeing his experience through the images became, I believe, a way for him to glimpse the meaning of it. Seeing and meaning became linked together. Finally, when the poem contained just the two images, I remember Elliott was more than satisfied. He was certain. He had his remembrances of Princeton. He had the remembrances that mattered. I sense he chose the word *remembrances* for the poem's title because he wanted to evoke, as one definition says, "something that serves to bring to mind or keep in mind some place, person, event, etc.; memento." Memento, as I looked more deeply, was once used as a word meant for giving warning. Elliott's images, while evoking the simplicity of his time in Princeton were also a warning of the complexity just ahead—for him, years of what he referred to as hiding as a gay man in a straight city—and for Einstein, the dark gravity of atomic energy research and where it would lead. The way Elliott saw his remembrances shifted because of the way he allowed himself to see—and reflect on—his images. Once he could see—and see all that the images contained—the poem came together easily.

Elliott's construction of "Remembrances of Princeton" was the beginning of my understanding that if we are willing to look closely, we'll not only see, but see *into* our images, and this seeing can lead us often to a deeper remembering as well as to what our images mean. Further, our images invite us into conversation with them. I think he dedicated this poem to Sister Miriam as a way of talking to her—and reconnecting with her. Several months after he finished the poem, when he feared his health was deteriorating even more, he returned to Baltimore to be near Sister Miriam and the hospice she served. The poem led him to insight about not only what he wanted the art to say, but also how he wanted to live out his life. When he had another stroke just a few months after his return to the States, Miriam sat peacefully at his side. I was lucky to sit together with them during Elliott's final days.

Seeing What Matters

I've used "Remembrances of Princeton"—and my witnessing of how Elliott created it—to help writers explore the dynamic relationship between text and image. I saw how carefully Elliott recorded image in his mind and let his mind shape it—give it form. I wondered what it would be like for other writers to literally shape their seeing through language and line. I asked them to play with this—to draw as well as write their images. I wanted them to sketch with pencils and words—and I hoped that when drawing and writing were used to focus their attention, they could slide into a more generative or contextualized seeing. I've incorporated this into my practice for years—and more and more I am convinced that drawing is seeing. That through drawing we see—an unfiltered seeing that can be more thorough or clear or complete leads us to language that allows us to share it.

A model for me is Lynda Barry. In *What It Is*, she writes: "Something happens to my thinking when I start to draw. It becomes more like listening than formulating. While I move my pen, I hear sentences, like this one for example. Spoken internally from one part of me to another. . ." (2008, 157). She calls it listening, but I experience it is as a way of attending, a way of seeing what the experience is. I thought writers could deliberately bring attention to seeing their images also.

Inspired by Betty Edwards' *Drawing from the Right Side of the Brain*, which encourages beginning drawers to focus on lines and recording them with their hand so what is seen is revealed as it is drawn, I have asked writers to engage in a similar process as they see into their own beautiful brevities—to follow the lines of what they see. They see visually and through word and then step back and reflect on what's revealed to them. I've also asked writers to see first—to focus on what they see or bring up an image in their mind and see it, really look at it, maybe also to draw it, before they write it, so all the details of their seeing are available to them before they write.

Barry also says that "the ordinary is extraordinary" (2008, 164) and that placing oneself within an image through writing, drawing, and/or humor allows for discovery of the "aliveness" of the image and one's experience or memory. In "Beautiful Brevities," this happens relationally. Elliott connects he and Einstein to a moment in time and what it portends; the connection gives context that allows us to see beyond them, to also glimpse history and culture.

I draw more and more on graphic memoirists and novelists, visual essayists, like Barry, MariNaomi (*Kiss and Tell* and *I Thought You Loved Me*) and Maira Kalman, (*The Principles of Uncertainty* and *And the Pursuit of Happiness*) among others, to teach writers where seeing and memory can intersect and where seeing can lead them. One thing I enjoy about Maira Kalman is she also walks a lot. For an interview for Slate.com, she says walking is time for "looking and not thinking;" back in her studio she can work with what she's seen (Alam 2020). Seeing via observation and distraction (a willingness to let the eye go where it wants to go) also leads her to stories from the dailyness around her or memories that bridge today and history, the present and the past. Telling stories "makes sense" to her, but she says she doesn't want to "tell the story that I seem to be telling. I want to tell you the understory. The not-story" (Schaffner 2010, 71).

Elliott seemed to prefigure the vital seeing and telling that is part of current graphic work and other burgeoning forms. He intuitively seemed to sense the personal and creative value of seeing and seeing into his own mind. His careful and clear seeing allowed the images from his past to be alive again—as living images, they spoke to him and he not only got to reconnect with his experience but to more fully realize it. From him, I learned—

Seeing leads to
Seeing into, which leads to
Seeing what matters.

Seeing Image Matters

In poems such as "The Red Wheelbarrow" by William Carlos Williams we see the image first. Williams focuses our attention on the red wheelbarrow and asks us to visualize the rainwater and white chickens. It is only once we are holding the image in our minds that we ask ourselves what does it mean that so much depends on these things? It wasn't until I started re-writing this piece that I sensed my first inkling of the relationship between seeing and imaging (seeing into image) may have been planted when I read "The Red Wheelbarrow" as a student. The explicitness of Elliott's process then fueled my thinking.

The Red Wheelbarrow
so much depends
upon

a red wheel
barrow
glazed with rain
water
beside the white
chickens

Lynda Barry seems to affirm this process of seeing first when she says, "Place yourself in the image and look around," (2008, 143) suggesting that by looking, we'll actually see. But my experience is that if we are seeing, we can train ourselves to also see into—and that will have positive benefit on what we ultimately create. In *A Sense of Self: Memory, The Brain and Who We Are*, Veronica O'Keane writes, "What we call a sense is also a memory: seeing is both the immediacy of the sight of the object and the identification of the image" (2021, 27). For me, she is affirming that when we recognize the image (object), we also connect to it, allowing us to see it and associate with it.

Elliott did that when he remembered Princeton, and I realize that is what I have been doing as I've worked through my memories of my time with him. To test my remembrances or help me find clarity or be more articulate, I'd simply asked myself, "What do you see?"

Usually, it was Elliott stretched out on his long bed, pillow propping up his back, his hand slapping his leg in insight or enjoyment—a gesture he made when he got to the punch line of a story. I'd nod my head and keep looking into the past, trying to genuinely see. The process has given me a remembrance—and memento of Elliott—a positive warning, if you will, that so much depends on my willingness to see.

II: Drastic Recounting: A Triptych of Loss and Not Found

Driving with Michael (Panel 1)

Google Maps: Oxford Station
Park End St, Oxford OX1 1HS, UK
Take Loverose Way to Park End St/A420
Continue on A420. Drive from Bayswater Rd, Mill St and B4011 to Buckinghamshire

Stephanie and I took the train from London Paddington to Oxford Station. We were morning travelers, part of the mid-week of everyday life. Commuters rushed or zoned out on the train, students walked or biked to classes, small children slept in prams or held hands with parents on their way to pre-schools or daycare, shops sold bacon sandwiches or scones with jam—and everyone, including us, slurped hot tea or coffee. It might have been Wednesday but, whatever the day, the route was the same. The National Rail schedule seems similar, if not the same, as it was in 1978–79. Trains, London Paddington to Oxford Station, are twice an hour much of the day, London Paddington to Oxford Station, 49 minutes with a stop in Reading, 52–54 minutes with a stop in Didcot, no train change.

Michael, who lived in Oxford, picked us up at the station. He didn't consult a map (no smart phones then, of course) or ask directions. He knew the way. One of us sat in the back and one up front with him. Google Maps says 14.7 miles; travel time: 32 minutes. In my mind, the drive was farther than that. Beyond Headington Hill, the road was narrow and twisty. The roundabouts were (and still are) a mystery to me. Michael entered each one, taking his turn, no indecision or insecurity, a quiet conversation between us or soft music, and we journeyed on.

> *At the roundabout, take the 1st exit onto St Clement's St/A420*
> *Use the left 2 lanes to turn slightly left onto Bayswater Rd*
> *Turn right onto B4027*
> *Turn left onto Pound Ln*
> *Pound Ln turns left and becomes Mill St*
> *Turn right on Oxford Road*

I loved the ride. The car itself was dark—at least the interior was— comfortable and muted. Muted, not to tamp things down (the work sessions were very alive), but because it was an honor to be invited at all. I understood two things were happening—we were getting the chance to do something that not everyone did and Michael really wanted Elliott to have students to engage with. Stephanie and I were the ones selected for that; in part, because we were writing poetry; in part, I am not sure why, except I'd already been meeting with Elliott informally. The car felt large, like luxury to me. Like so many things from that time, I have an impression, less a memory than a moment of seeing. I am reminded of Veronica O'Keefe again. My seeing is feeling here and I am following that. I'm trusting that if I follow what is visible to me and try to record it, I'll get somewhere with the writing.

Only now do I realize our meetings also gave Michael a chance to be with Elliott, not as friend or caretaker, but as writer and teacher; he also got to share his work with Elliott (and us). I can hear Elliott delighting in Michael's poetry, praising his novel, which Michael didn't talk about, and starting to say something about Michael's Irish American lineage but stopping himself. The youngest in the room I kept lots of questions to myself. Stories shared related to what we were making. Mostly, our work was our way of knowing each other.

Michael was strong and durable, Elliott thinning and physically fragile, but when they spoke across the room to each other, you couldn't tell who would live a long time and who wouldn't. The moment—and what they had to say to each other—held them. It transcended age and health. I want to show it to you, but as I reach into memory the care I sensed between them short-circuits my vision; sometimes what we see is feeling so I recount that. I am aware the past is so present in this writing; my awareness of it and the limits of what I can see in it shape what I can say.

Michael and Elliott were mentors to us, and, at the same time, were learners with us; all these years later I'm still sorting out the gift of that. It is hard to describe how peaceful our work together in Chilton House was. Elliott may have been the bigger personality in the room, but the space and the sessions supported all of us. The experience we shared was there for us even when we were not together. We carried it with us until we gathered again the next week. Clearly, I still carry it now.

I track the turns and the photos of the route Google offers, but, again, it's ritual, not ride, I see. For me, it was better to be a passenger, to look out the windows—and within the car—and take it all in. For an hour or two every week, Chilton was a refuge, a home for us—not collectively, but for each of us individually; that doesn't mean we all didn't take a lot from it, the opposite. We were all in the midst of significant change but didn't know it yet or weren't acknowledging it. As writer, I think of ritual as a repeatable inquiry into memory. Inside the moments I probe aren't lessons but experience, like the friendship between Michael and Elliott, that I can refer to, try to see accurately, and let bolster me.

Slight left onto Manor Rd
Turn right onto Bicester Rd/B4011
Take Brill Rd to Thame Rd in Chilton
3 min (1.3 mi)
Turn right onto Brill Rd

Brill Rd turns right and becomes Thame Rd
   Chilton House
Chilton, Aylesbury HP18 9LR, UK

We arrived—and I only remember what I can see: The front of the building and Elliott's room. Elliott's bed was not in the center of his room but farther in. There was an end table with a small lamp on his left side. We sat to his right. I am seeing how much my memory of the place and Elliott's room is in what Elliott wrote about it: the white room, the avocado dome, the large window he could look out of. What he wanted us to see. I don't see the armoire with closed doors and hidden drawers or the small bathroom with a sometimes-open door that was never used during our visits. I did not keep a journal or record of our tutorials in any systematic way. I did not take photos, never one of him or any of us. We were not yet a constant photo-taking culture. I want to set the scene, remember the moment, our arrivals and departures, but in many ways it's all blurred, not to one, but onto a fuzzy loop of impressions that keeps playing. I want to see it all again—but I don't know if I can. Again, the work seems to be pursuing the memory and what to make of that, not finding it. I can stay with it—or set it aside. My choice is to trust the pursuit and see what emerges.

In my mind, I step inside Eliott's room—and I see Michael already through the door. His presence slight, on the periphery, but he was very present. So much of the experience I had of Eliott—after I introduced myself to him on my own—was because of Michael. And it bothers me that I can only see moments, can't recount him. What I see are his long legs crossed, him comfortable in a padded chair, okay with whatever is next.

Two more images:

Michael and I sit in a kitchen nook, his wife in and out of the conversation, Irish whiskey, shot glasses on the table. The nook is wood, not forgiving at all for a man as tall as him. He takes up every bit of the bench he sits on. I sit on a small wooden chair with a padded seat and an open back. The whiskey is smooth, easy to drink. There is the same calm as in Elliott's room. I can hear part of a sentence—the words *beauty* and *John Donne* come to me but the rest is lost.

Michael and I stand just inside the doorway to the program office at the Antioch Centre for British Studies on Danbury Street, me pages to type up in my hands, him stressed because Antioch, in massive financial crisis, has not paid him for almost two months. He wears a beige raincoat and carries a well-used leather briefcase. Sunlight streams in; the room feels very white. He leans in a bit to tell me that when I graduate, I need to get a doctorate. I try to hear the words but I only remember the gist: You are young—here I am in mid-life having to get one to keep teaching or to get work.

The message is do it now. And I do, Michael and Elliott support my application.

What I could see is defined by what I could know. What I sensed, however, was he really wanted Elliott to stay in England. But Elliott would decide to leave, and when he did, Michael and I wouldn't process it; I don't remember us ever speaking about why Elliott returned to Baltimore.

When Elliott dies, I lose Michael too. I don't think I have been in touch with him since I left London in 1979. I can't remember any reason we did not stay in touch except too much change and too much loss. I am sorry for the loss of him—and now so sorry that I've lost how and why that happened. That's another loss.

I vaguely search for him on the internet. I find a reference to France, a poem, and an exhibit and art book (that seems like him)—and that's all there is or at least all that's easy to find. I don't want to keep looking. If he wanted to be found, he'd have a presence. He was good to me, and our relationship, like many, was a moment in time, one that did not extend past Elliott's death. When I left London, there was no way to close the gap between where I lived and Michael moved to, no bridge between the Elliott who left me and the Elliott who left him. His relationship with Elliott was long, very different than mine; what we shared was a desire to help keep him alive, and neither of us succeeded at that. It felt like failure to me, maybe it did to him too. Maybe that was too much to overcome or we just moved on.

I began this recounting because I wanted to re-find Michael; I am not sure why. But as I stay with the moments and glimpses of memory, I reconnect with how he helped me become who I am. I lost my connection to him but not to what he gave me as person and writer. That is mine to hold onto and draw from whenever I am willing to see it.

Sister Miriam (Panel 2)

I am struck by how few details I have—I can't remember the name of Sister Miriam's order or the hospice it ran where Elliott lived (Stella Maris,

I find it on the internet). I have only the certainty of what I see: The stark white of the room in the hospice, the pristine white sheets, the thin narrow bed, and Elliott no longer able to speak, breathing and breathing and breathing, in rhythm but with restraint. His chest rises—up and down—nothing else moves. The bed has a dark railing, and I am sitting next to it in a white chair. The room is dusty white, there is gray light. Sister Miriam is there, hair pulled back, her habit and headpiece white, her presence, a comfort, the soft wrinkles on her face and hands soften her and the space. She eases everything.

In contrast, at Elliott's memorial service, I wear a V-neck sweater of black, turquoise, and white, a straight, mid-length black skirt, and black suede backless heels. I know Sister Miriam was there—but my mind holds only the space, the room full, the standing podium and microphone. I can't see anyone as I speak. What I can see is her worry for me.

She stands in a white corner near the bed, a rough sound catches in Elliott's throat. Her stillness radiates care—for him and for me, even as she tells me: He didn't want you to see him like this. She isn't suggesting I am not welcome or should leave. She knows I won't, that I am with him too—that what will happen next will devastate me but for the moment I am all in. She helps to make that possible for me. She says it to acknowledge Elliott, what he said but not what he meant; to be clear she knows and she understands he needs me as I need him—or at least I think that. I sit with him for a week. The call saying he has died comes a day after I had to leave.

When I wrote about Elliott creating "beautiful brevities" more than twelve years ago, my father was in end-stage Alzheimer's—and I was balancing my experiences of death, my father's impending death, and all that I learned from Elliott as I wrote. I focused on what I found in Elliott in that earlier piece—and what I could carry forward—but not on what I lost from him, not on his death. Perhaps that was because I knew soon death would be immediate and very real for me again—and I was looking for life in what I wrote or just trying to forestall the dismantling effects loss brings with it. Now, I can depict that moment in time and all that arises from it more complexly.

Sister Miriam resonated kindness and may have been the kindest person I ever met. She asked me to stay in touch with her. I did not, and that is a loss for me—and on me. I am disappointed in myself that when Elliott died, I let her and Michael go from my life so easily. But as I write this piece and realize there is more that needs to be said now, Sister

Miriam is a touchstone I return to. I try to see her or at least see through her. She shows me my relationship with Elliott includes those who came with him—that the depth of care they had for him is a lesson but so is that it also included me. I have been writing my way through these images to find that. The lessons I've learned from Elliott include them.

Sister Miriam was Elliott's tangible link to death, really his death guide, so he needed to get closer to her so he could get there. In "Surety" (Coleman 1989, 21), Elliott writes to death. Soon after he finished this poem, he left Chilton and moved back to Baltimore.

Surety

Hydrogen
Are you there?
Are you there?
I am not sure

Oxygen
Are you there?
Not sure

I submerge in real water
and come up for air
unsure

Death
Are you here?
You are here!
Blackness
Sure
Sure

Elliott's Drastic Recounting (Panel 3)

Four Counties of Youth:
A Fiction

I was born in Broome County, New
York state in 1906. There I swam

the Chenango River, climbed the
Appalachian Mountains, and
memorized Vergil.

At 17, I went to DuPage County,
Illinois to work my way through
college. I shoveled cement,
waited on table, played in a
dance band, played a pipe organ,
sold shoes, life insurance, and
potatoes from the Red River
Valley. One winter: from a
stand at the Northwestern
Station, I drove a yellow taxi-
cab nights. I loved the un-
American Northwestern Railroad.
Its orange-colored cars smashed
through on the left hand side
of the roadbed. The first year
in DuPage was a great year. I
would get up early, do 100
pushups, splash in and out of
a cold tub, towel off and
smoke a Chesterfield cigarette,
down a tomato juice, and get
to the courthouse for the
murder trials. Noon I would
run down to Milner's
Restaurant and hold a table
for the Defense attorney. He
liked to sit alone. While he
read the menu, I watched his
steel-blue eyes. He gave his
order. I brought his lunch.
Next morning, I was back at
the courthouse. His name was
Clarence Darrow. He got his
murderer off.

At 21, I went to work in Buncombe
County, North Carolina. The French
Broad River cut through the Blue
Ridge and emptied into the
Mississippi. A U.S. senator,
it was said, authorized a bill
to dredge the French Broad
deep enough for ocean vessels
to enter the Buncombe pink
beds. When laughed at in Washington,
he rejoined: "I was just talking
to Buncombe." There was a U.S.
Calvary post in Buncombe.
Captain Rathjen was in charge.
I joined the post to learn
to jump. One night, when
my horse had refused the
triple bar twice, I heard
the Captain's voice: "Mr.
Coleman, take my horse."
He had a big white horse of
which he kept close care. I
thanked him by flying over
the hurdle. I thank him still.

At 24 I went down to the Outer
Banks of North Carolina to swim
in the surf, and I stayed on.
Dr. Johnston was the only
surgeon in Dare County. When
he had an emergency, he would
pick me up in a small plane, and
we would fly to Hatteras
and land on the beach. While
he operated in the Coast Guard
station, I would drag aside
the driftwood from the nose
of the plane to be ready

for takeoff to Kitty Hawk.
Dare was the best of the
Counties. It left a sad
memory: The suicide note
of a Dare County youth, "I
wish I could have been a
homosexual like Jesus was."

Youth over, I went to New York
City. I loved Manhattan Island.
I loved my job. I loved Jones
Beach. I love my flat. And
I loved my Freudian psycho-
analysis. I found I had been
a Gay through all the counties
of youth without admitting it
or believing it. Before analysis
was over, I had experienced 200
homosexual encounters on
Manhattan Island without catching
a sexual disease or meeting a
lover. War II came. I tried
to enlist in the U.S. Navy
and was rejected for bad
eyesight. New York was a
nowhere. Another job flashed
from another city. It was a
straight city. I went there
and tried to be a Straight.
Then, in love with my new job,
I gave up sex for years and
was elected to *Who's Who in
In America.*

I have drastically recounted
Four Counties of Youth to
Stephanie Weller, asking that
she send copies to twelve other
writers:

A.R. Ammons
Russell Baker
Eugene Barenburg
John Barth
Josephine Jacobsen
Rigg Kennedy
John Leax
Michael Lynch
Richard O'Connell
K.S. Polistina
Louis D. Rubin
Cindy Shearer

New Year's 1979

Elliott's poem, "Four Counties of Youth" (1980, 15–20) is a curated record of his life but became a vehicle for leaving, not just England and Michael and me, but his life. I think the poem carried him—or at least cracked open the door—to death.

I don't remember when he began writing *Four Counties of Youth* or when he began to talk about it as his final book. I can see Stephanie, who was a few years older than me, no face visible just her blond/brown curls, hunched in a dark wood chair writing each word. The poems were created one by one—and, at some point, Elliott said they were or they just became a collection. He did not tell us why the poem "Four Counties of Youth" or any others in the collection mattered; he let the poems tell us themselves. That was a lesson he offered me—to let the work speak. It was fine to let others into the writing process, but the work supported and spoke for itself.

What I remember is Elliott having to convey it, tell it all. I do not know how much our work together gave Elliott what he may have wanted or needed to create it. I believe that being able to write and revise it with us sitting together with him allowed for a re-sensing, a way of engaging memory in a more resonant way, that helped him to deliver his life to us as he wanted us to see it: Choosing what to leave in and what to leave out. Choosing what he wanted to name and what he did not.

The word *drastically* may be the most important in the poem. For me, "Four Counties of Youth" is reclamation, if not liberation. His choices reflect what he wants the poem to be. It does not hesitate; the simple, declarative sentences ask us to see; it does not over speak. The words and sentences have a relationship, are resonant with each other, except when he says he has "drastically" recounted his four counties of youth; that choice is deliberate. It vibrates beyond itself. He is calling attention to the word—a way of calling it out—and through it meaning he intends a strong or far-reaching effect that touches us sonically and emotionally. He is writing to people he has known—many he has worked with—for years and years. For Elliott, every word counts, has a reason, and contributes to (a) the drastic effect and (b) the recounting of his life. Recounting can mean to tell someone something or narrate an event or experience, but the origins of the word (from Old Northern French *reconter*) can also suggest re-telling, as if telling again. I love how Elliott plays with this, and through it, us. The telling or accounting is new for us, but for him (since he recounted his experiences to himself for a long time, making choices about what to tell), the poem is a re-construction, a telling again. The reconstructing is also a reclaiming of who he is. The word *drastically* is for him and for us. Before he dies, I believe he understands, he has to be willing to recount himself to himself more accurately or closer to the facts/events as he knows them so that he can tell us. The "fiction" is not what is shared but has been not said or was hidden or left out.

Elliott believes there is drastic effect—so warns us of this directly. Of course, the warning comes at the end of the poem; we get it after we have read it. Another way of playing with us. He is also warning himself; as he finishes the poem, the reality of his re-telling as new telling shifts what all those on the list or anyone who reads the poem will know about him and/ or what he can tell them about who he is. I sense him calling himself out—as he comes out. There are almost no words of emotion in the poem—just subject, active verb, object. So *drastically* can resonate effect. This is why I think resonance is so important here; it offers visual vibrational space for the work to live.

He dates the poem as New Year's 1979. Elliott is seeing his way to death. I sense he lists that day to show he is also resonating with the ways the world is changing (from one year to the next, from one time to another, from some attitudes or perspectives to others)—and that he won't be there to change with it. He wrote the poem ten years after the Stonewall Uprising, and two years before the first reported cases of AIDS. What others experienced and what they would experience seemed beyond him. What he could do was drastically recount his life, making sure there was a record of it. *Dick Clark's New Year's Rockin' Eve* in 1979 featured the first countdown to midnight in Times Square. Perhaps while Elliott wrote the final words of the poem, he felt the clock shift, the ball drop, lives and cultures in motion.

Again, Elliott, as he does in "Beautiful Brevities," is making us see as we read. In this poem, seeing in (seeing into the moment) leads to seeing out (beyond him and into the culture). For me, that's resonance; as we look into his life, our view expands/vibrates out—connecting us to events and experiences beyond him and beyond us. Using visual words to make readers see is always a goal in certain ways for him, but in this poem, he really wanted his chosen readers—and by extension everyone else—to see, to understand, regardless of how it felt.

How much of who and what we are is our work? This is a question that, for me, seems embedded in much of Elliott's work and requires this recounting. I think when Elliott recited "Four Counties of Youth" to Stephanie with all of us listening as witnesses, it released him. It generated resonance for him and for us.

I think he hoped for resonance, even though he would likely have said he was reporting, and wanting to extend the range of our vision, making us see him, and, through him, differently. In *The Art of Resonance*, writer/director Anne Bogart says, "Resonant art awakens and casts light into the hidden realities of our lives and of our world … [Resonance] exists in between consonance and dissonance and does nothing less than challenge one's own identity and assumptions" (2021, 11). Like a well-crafted musical instrument, Elliott's visual words echo and vibrate, enriching and maybe amplifying the connection between him and us, between then and now. I resonate with that—a phrase used often in California—feels true as we read.

I learned from Elliott that how we bring ourselves into our writing is a series of choices—how much to reveal and what to tell. In this poem, Elliott in context, via perspective, using visual words, helps us to see: as one dictionary definition says, "be conscious of what is around you by using your eyes."

I got the chance to see how those choices shaped the work. Choice, I learned, is based, in part, on what we see (and so can know) in any given moment—and, to a large degree, what we resonate with and can or are willing to claim.

I don't remember how many times we met but after the holidays; Elliott was making his plan to leave. I knew him such a short time—summer of 1978 to winter 1980. The resonance was strong and then it was lost.

I know him through the poetry—through what he created and shared—and that, less than what it could have been, is a lot. I can't tell you too much more about him. What I can tell is what I continue to take from him. It has taken me most of my life to understand maybe the most important thing I found in my relationship with him—loss is not failure—it is loss.

The loss of Elliott for me is not from his work. There is a lot found there, and I have embedded it in my life. The loss is of the person, the one I cared for and wanted to know and learn more from, of not knowing I could still carry him with me, something I would have benefitted from when, in a few years, my mother would die. I had choices, more than one option; I limited myself and what I could create because I couldn't take that in.

I did see what Elliott was struggling with. A fear of death floated through every moment he tried to be alive, in the struggle to accept that he was not entirely who he thought or hoped he was. I ventured into his life in a moment of loss and loss for him, and I was a moment of found for him as he was for me—so what I have shared comes out of that context.

Four Counties of Youth is a book of poetry as well as poem. When Elliott left Chilton, he gave me his poems and asked me to publish his last book. I did. I sent the published book to all the people I could think of and, of course, to all on his list. Then I sent it to libraries. While working on this book, I did a search and found a copy via my public library system in California. The book was in Southern California; it had been in storage for years—I requested it. I am not sure why, except to see that it had life beyond me. I held it in my hands, read the poems, and turned the pages. It was the same as the copy I own, except it had a sticker on the cover saying that I'd have to pay $115 if I damaged the book in any way. I sent it back intact. I hope that if someone in another forty-five years tries to read it, it will still be there for them.

III: Found: Imagining

In 1995, I came back to Chilton. I think of it as a pilgrimage but one on the left side of the road in a blue Mini Cooper with my five-year-old son. I was thirty-eight years old, recently divorced. The idea was to see again the place where I had known Elliott. I was struggling as a writer—actually,

I'd pretty much quit writing, perhaps I thought if saw Chilton again I'd re-find what the place had given me via Elliott (and Michael) all those years ago—or at least tap into it. For me, the pilgrimage was a chance to re-connect—and my son was up for the adventure. It was intentional journey, in which the realities of parenting came with me. I was hoping the place holding the story I had lived was still there. The person I was had left. The relationships had gone away. If the place was still there, then maybe something I'd experienced was still there too.

My focus was making it fun for my young son. I never drove when I lived in England. I was curious to take on the roads we traveled with Michael and experience them anew.

I rented the car in Oxford. I wasn't brave or ambitious enough to drive from London. It's fun to remember that at that time I drove the stick shift easily—and I think for half a minute that impressed my son. Inside he got to sit on the left side in a somewhat roomy black vinyl seat, and with his right hand, he could reach the gear shift and pretend he was driving. The car was thin and rounded like a tin can, the wood veneer dashboard felt like a small bit of luxury. On the back roads, it was mostly just us and we rode with the windows all the way down. Maps, not GPS, got us there. We pulled into the long dirt driveway—I didn't remember there was a driveway at all—and saw the large historic house. I knew we were at the right place right away. Unlike me, it had not changed at all.

I had a photo once—I don't know where it is—what I recall is Chiton House and a dirt patch where we parked the car—that's it. I am very surprised when I search the internet and see the many buildings and the large grounds. I don't remember them. Memory jarred—I start looking for resources to re-see/re-vision Chilton—my image of a contained place clearly an illusion. I find the Bucks Garden Trust Report. Historic features include the South Pavilion, the former kitchen garden, the North Pavilion, Upper Lawn, Park, and Pond in Woodland (Bucks Garden Report 2019, 11); the map lists fourteen different areas. In "Entrances and Approaches," the report says, "the private tarmac drive extends between plain stone gate piers with pyramidal caps" and ". . .continues north shaded by mature limes for 80m" (2019, 5). Since 1945, Chilton House has been a nursing home (2019, 6).

I had no idea all that was there, but I did remember Elliott told us the vicar had come to visit him. I'm not sure if the vicar came on his own or if someone at Chilton House invited him to visit. What I realize now is there was a Chilton developing inside Elliott that mapped to what was outside his window and its history. The narrative Elliott creates in his poem "Chilton" arises from the narrative that the house and the grounds convey and how it began to live in him.

I visited Chilton House so many times, not really seeing anything, and Elliott could look out his window—and see so much more. Elliott, for the most part, did not leave his room. Our route was simple: We went from car to Elliott's room and back to car again and again. Tunnel experience—so tunnel vision—but not for Elliott. All of Chilton was alive for him.

A nursing home masquerading as manor house. I do not know why I was not more curious about this place we visited, except the place was linked to Elliott in my mind—it was no more, no less than that. Elliott, too, didn't need the actual Chilton; he just needed to let it help him imagine—and it did. In the end, the stories within Chilton became his to make and tell.

I stepped out of the Mini Cooper but stayed by it. I didn't walk across the large lawn and up to the also large front door. I did need to remember the place was there—that I did visit—that Elliott had been there.

I looked at Chilton House carefully. My son, realizing this was all there was to see, made it clear he was ready to leave. I told him, yes, we were ready to go. It was a short pilgrimage. For a moment, I'd succeeded in bringing past and present together. This time I took Chilton House, not Elliott, with me.

Nigel Coates in *Narrative Architecture* speaks to how we can carry psychological experience or "traces" of one space as we move into another (2012, 27–28). I know right away when I read this section that Elliott's poem "Chilton" is an embodiment of one space physically and psychologically lingering in another, but I can't find what I am reaching for.

So I make a postcard, a form/medium that years ago I worked with a lot. I know it will help me find my way. In service of this book, I make a one-sided postcard, text, image, and stamp all on the same side, rather than image on one side, text and stamp on the other.

I take the blank card. I want to cut up an image of Chilton, and I realize I need a better pair of scissors to get the fine lines of the cut right. I go to my art space to look for materials. When I open the drawer to look for scissors, I see it—two sheets of handmade paper from another project— one fuchsia red, the one pink/rose. I know right way what I want to do. I get the scissors and a thin knife, and I cut away. I cut out a version of Chilton House in red paper and then I begin to cut away the building— first windows on various floors and the "stone dressings." I realize we need to see into the building, but the red paper is a barrier—an attractive one but it needs to suggest, not show, us there is more inside. I cut out phrases from the report and part of the grass. I leave a hint of the dirt driveway that leads to the front door. I cut out the front door—we could walk right in—but what would we be able to see?

I make a stamp—cut out words from the report "a fine example," a "Tudor manor house;" the theme of "interest" runs through the postcard—history, artistic, architectural, archaeological. I replace stone dressings as phrases from the report, form the boundaries of the stamp. I put cut-out windows on the stamp. Along the driveway, I place a pink/rose flap, a message inside, but the Chilton House banner covers it—you'd have to break it to read the message—what you can see—"important things I found in my . . . with him—loss is not failure—it is loss."

The card, of course, is for me—I am creating it—trying to find my way—but the message is for Elliott—"I can still see you there."

I know he is in his room.

Chilton House was rectangular and boxy, but Elliott's room had two things that, I feel, he connected with. It was elongated and quiet—Elliott could feel as if he could move, even if he didn't much without help. Also,

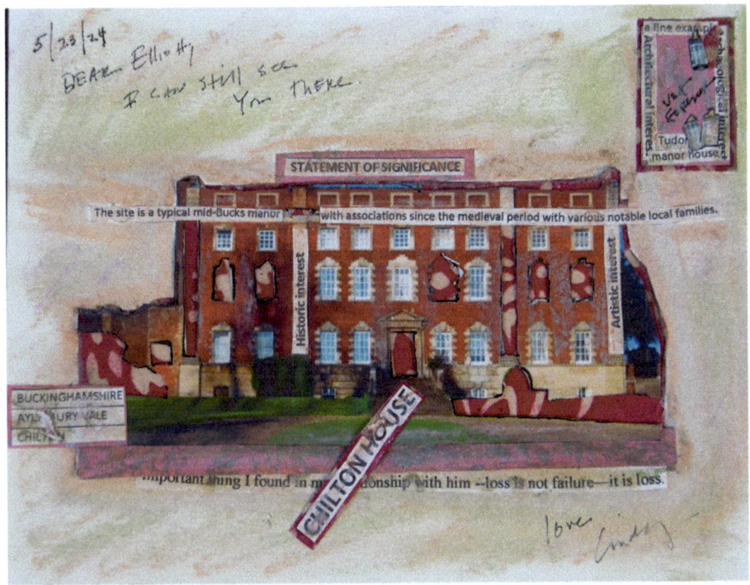

FIGURE 1 *Chilton House*, Postcard, 6" x 8", 2024.
Mixed Media paper, handmade paper, oil pastels, printed paper, black marker

there were windows that let him look outside; without leaving his bed, he could easily see beyond the house. Inside the cocoon of his room, his mind could place him anywhere on the land he wanted to be. He could reference it any way he wanted via history, architecture, his poetry, the church. He could stay in "right now"—or he could travel to any time he wanted to. The place invited imagination. Overhearing becomes a real and imagined thing, a method for his writing.

Through the postcard, I find the narrative between space and time—or, as Coates might say, to associate to or imagine what I have to say (2012, 32).

I do not remember driving up to the front of the building when Stephanie, Michael and I visited. Maybe we used the back entrance, but I don't think so. I see a small glimmer of white shirts and dark skirts, dishes lifted from tables, the sounds of silverware clanging—like we walked near a dining room on our way to the stairs. Somehow for me it was a solitary building— occupying a space and one place inside—Elliott's room. The image of it has not changed. The space dims only when Elliott's time with us ends.

Traces of the place—both as it was and as I remember it (or as I have imagined it) stay with me.

Now I am aware it offered so much more for Elliott. It was the place, if only for a short time, he could imagine living.

Chilton is my favorite poem—I see the place when I read it. I do not remember much about how it was written or how we worked through drafts together. I remember Elliott became enamored of the idea of "overhearing." I didn't keep notes of the conversation or record what was said when we worked together—it wasn't that kind of thing. We weren't creating something for posterity or for us to return to—we were making work in the here and now.

What I remember is Elliott turned to us and said he was listening out the window a lot. Then he explained that he'd been listening to a BBC program, an interview—I don't remember if it was about science or philosophy or religion—and he now understood "overhearing." Elliott was very taken with it. It enlivened him to talk about it. Except for John Paul II, I hadn't seen him so interested in anything. I have scoured the internet, without success, to see if I could a find a BBC program from the fall of 1978 in which overhearing was an important concept.

Overhearing, I believe, was hearing everything but also being able to discern it, hearing within and between, all the layers, past and present, history and the moment right now. If I play with the way that Coates refers to narrative "genus" in architecture (2012, 81), I think that overhearing is not a binary experience, but what I think Coates might call a "biotope." He says it can "destabilize the physical reality of territory, therefore allowing it to be open to multiple interpretations. . ." (Coates 2012, 100). Perhaps it is an interplay between real and imagined, fact and fabrication, associations and discoveries, physical and spiritual with being, remembering, integrating and creating. As writer, Elliott took the concept of overhearing and captured it for himself, and he wrote "Chilton."

Here's what I remember: He was animated—he didn't have to say it—but for a moment, having to face death, if he could just be part of everything, hearing, at the same time, what was in front of him and hearing what was beyond him, he would be part of it all—rather than at the end—if not a perpetual beginning, at least an ongoing conversation.

The poem is my ongoing connection to him. More than any other poem in *Four Counties of Youth*, Elliott let himself stop being in memory and let himself be in the present (Coleman 1980, 10–11). From there he could look back or look out or beyond. Chilton reminds me that we can always imagine our way to what we want to say, maybe that is the best and most direct route.

When I read this poem, Elliott is always re-found for me. The Elliott I could know, the one on the page, the one I could carry forward. Not the dead one, not the loss. Each time it is dark and morning, dark and day.

Chilton

1.

The question of Chilton was the same question
all other houses had asked him:
Whether to live or die.
                    He had not heard them.
When Michael Lynch drove him out one morning
to meet Mrs. Morrison and see Chilton,
he was stirred.
Half-blind unbeliever,
he stayed at the foot of the stairs
he could not climb.
The height, the somber face of Chilton
silenced him into the stillness.
                    A few flowers moved.

Michael was back; there was a back entrance.
Was it the age of the place that quickened him?
He hated old places.
But the halls,
the white-sculptured linen walls of a room
and its avocado dome
and a view of the village
made him want to stay.
The day was Mrs. Morrison's. She ordered a shower built.

2.

What if some sixteenth century sounds he hated
abused the open window?

Could he not just overhear them?
Overhear everything?
Overhear it all?
The answer of Chilton was a spatial answer
A murmur of bricks
A whisper of bricks
The scythe of the wind
The radiant whisper of space

On an autumn afternoon at about sunset,
somebody began to ring the Chilton bells.
The changes were cheerful.
They rang half an hour.
When they ended, as from far off,
a single chime began to reply.

Later, he met the Vicar. He said the church
had some medieval stone.

3.

On a winter night in 1979,
when it had cooled down to 2 degrees below
absolute zero,

the Church of St. Mary the Virgin, Chilton
exploded.
Peter the Vicar heard it.
Director Joan Morrison heard it.
Michael, the poet, heard it.
Gilly, the cook in her black dress, heard it.
George, the artisan, heard it.
The girl Caroline heard it.
Each of them had been listening for something.
I overheard it because I had been overhearing it,
off and on,
for 4 billion years.

The nave was hydrogen light.
The chancel was voices.
Saxon voices
Roman voices
Norman voices
Elizabethan voices
Modern voices
Young voices
Then it was dark and morning,
                              dark and day.

IV: Found and Loss, Not Quite Found

2014

I enter the yellow room.

I am in the south drawing room of Sir John Soane's house, now museum, in Holborn. In 1833, Soane, a wealthy British architect, secured an Act of Parliament, which, in perpetuity, preserved his house as it was at the time of his death.

I am here because a colleague, an expert in eighteenth-century domestic spaces, tells me Soane painted the room its vibrant yellow simply because he could. In "The Most Modern 18th-Century Room You've Ever Seen," Elizabeth Anne Hartmann (2016) reports the yellow paint used here was one of the first that didn't oxidize and turn black;

British designer Tim Gosling tells her, "The spectacle of walking into a room that glows yellow must have been extraordinary."

It is.

The yellow is a little more muted than when the room is well photographed (please do look at a photograph), the day is overcast, but the spectacle is still there. The inviting yellow is everywhere.

To me, it also suggests another yellow room. My bedroom (circa 1973) on Hubbard Drive.

Like Soane, I made my room yellow because I could. He got access to more enduring paint, now called Soanian yellow (Soane Yellow SC429). I got coveted space. The yellow on yellow made it feel like it was more than yellow. It was yellow's yellow, electric lemon, a yellow brighter than daffodils, as sharp as sunshine.

Gosling also speaks to the feel of the room, the room's impression—how the use of one color for the walls, couch, and curtains, even the fireplace feels yellow—takes it out of its own time and makes it "contemporary."

Maybe. But for me, the repeated use of yellow acts as a singular voice, corralling multiple stories.

I look a long way back. In my yellow room, I am sixteen.

It will be five years before I travel to London, meet Elliott and Michael, live the stories that will later intertwine.

The room has two metal closet doors, painted yellow. The bookshelves bracketed to a yellow wall are also painted yellow.

The box springs and full-sized mattress sit on the floor pushed against another yellow wall. I have a window above my head and another near my feet so sunshine can cover me.

Wispy, see-through, yellow polka-dot curtains hang across the windows.

Yellow sheets, pillows cases, and duvet cover the mattress.

Like Soane, my impetuousness is one color—so the room speaks for itself.

The room also has an alcove, painted yellow. There is a wood desk inside it (I want to remember it as yellow, but did I paint it? I wonder if my mind is trying to color it now).

The floor lamp flagging the desk is absolutely yellow.

The room is upstairs and around the corner. It's an oasis or perhaps an island, separate from the rest of the house. The room was designated as my mother's sewing room, though she always did the mending downstairs in the gold chair in the TV room or on the white couch in the living room. It had also been deemed my father's office, but he worked in his actual office at another house (which he'd converted into office space) or at the dining room table in our house. For years the room was (mostly) unused, while my sister and I shared a room.

When she moved out, I announced I was moving to a room of my own.

I overtake it with yellow, a color that radiates. It says: This room will stand out.

In my mind, I see the yellow clearly, but I can't name it. There are hints of it in Chiura Obata's *Grand Canyon* and *The Enthronement Drum*, a cover for *Japan*. But like so many things (including my room), there is more to the color than what we see. I look for it in the chapter on yellow in Victoria Finlay's *Color: A Natural History of the Palette*. She writes gamboge is "the brightest yellow imaginable, almost fluorescent" (2004, 220), but it's not quite there, not my yellow.

Kassia St. Clair in *The Secret Lives of Color* (2016) shows me it could be Acid Yellow, the color of the original smiley face, or Chrome Yellow, the yellow of Van Gogh's sunflowers. But Soane's yellow is the only one I relate to, that connects me to what I've seen before.

Soane, Gosling tells Hartmann, wanted visitors to feel like they were in sunny Pompeii or Rome, including designing lanterns with yellow stained glass to add to the effect.

I don't remember much about my room, except the color. But in it, I did feel at ease like soft butter melting on toast or tart and sweet in the right ratio in lemon pound cake.

Hartmann writes, "Soane's cheekiness is in simplification" (2016). He trusted his instinct and choices. In my yellow room, I did too.

I've wanted to simplify the color of my time with Elliott. I don't know if I can find the cheek to do it. Instinct and choices don't feel so certain without paint.

Soon after all the poems in *Four Counites of Youth* were recorded, things shifted, maybe like in "Chilton," imploded. Stephanie left the program, and Antioch's financial chaos absorbed Michael. It seemed like our group tutorial lasted a long time, but it was just a few months.

I did visit Elliott on my own, a few times. Without a car, it was difficult to get to Chilton House. Google maps say from one hour and fifteen minutes to three hours thirty-six minutes from Oxford, not including the return travel. A whole day to travel to Chilton and back to London. I took the bus from Oxford to Thame —and then walked—or once I hitchhiked (I didn't have it in me to try that again).

"Cheek" seems needed when we radically narrow our options or settle into intention. For me, it seems unavoidable when we audaciously trust our choices. Soane asks for his to live in perpetuity. Reconnecting with mine is enough.

My yellow room, unlike Soane's, was a place and a moment in time. From it, I begin to understand color as a container, storytelling beyond words. Now, as was my time with Elliott, it's a touchstone, an object embedded with memories, a multi-layered, unresolved, circuitous guide.

I am in the yellow-gold kitchen of an artist-friend's house in Winter Park. It is probably 1983—Elliott died in 1980. When he left London in 1979, he said he'd be there for me. It is the first time, but not the last, I will feel this deep fatigue.

I sit at a small table with my friend, and her mother, a psychic. I am meeting her for the first time. We drink sweaty lemonade. The air is a weak yellow but heavy. My friend's mother says, " I don't usually do this, especially with someone I've just met, but there is a man sitting with you. He is all white—white skin, white hair, white beard—and he says he won't leave until I tell you he is still with you."

The gold tones in the room conflict with the stark white she says she sees. I nod my head, but I can't believe her. My experience is when someone dies they are not with you. They are gone. I resist the cheekiness in the simplification.

I step out of the Soane Museum and onto Lincoln's Inn Fields.

Elliott and I are alone in his room at Chilton House. I don't think he was expecting me. The sparse room is sparser. Things have been given away or are being packed up. The next time I see him he'll be dying in a Baltimore hospice with Sister Miriam at his side. Sunlight, reminiscent of a Mediterranean glow, catches the edge of his hand, and he reaches for something.

I spent too much time trying to understand yellow while writing this piece. I kept trying to connect Soane's room, mine, and Elliott through yellow. I kept learning more (adding information and details), while the piece was asking me—and I kept dodging the question—What does yellow mean to you? Finally, I saw it—for me, this piece was not only about what yellow is but about why Soane and I used it. The meaning, as it often is in writing, is in why, not what. When I got that, I could finally take in *cheekiness is in simplification*. I began to see how (1) trust (a form of surety) and mistrust/not being sure permeated the piece, and (2) trust is often, maybe inherently, cheekiness (an audacious act).

In London's gray-white light, I see this: Elliott, fearful in the dark, finds a white envelope on his mud-yellow nightstand; on it he writes, "love, Elliott."

The yellow room is past, but the surety within it is there for me. And the white envelope?

I make the slight right on Remnant Street and walk toward Holborn Tube. Maybe I have enough cheek now to just reimagine it.

Resources

Poems

Coleman, Elliott, *Four Counites of Youth*, Geryon Press, 1980.

Definitions

Image: https://www.etymonline.com/word/image#etymonline_v_1520
Memento: https://www.dictionary.com/browse/memento and https://www.etymonline.com/search?q=memento
Drastically: https://www.oxfordlearnersdictionaries.com/us/definition/english/drastically?q=drastically
Recounting: https://www.etymonline.com/search?q=recount
See: https://dictionary.cambridge.org/dictionary/english/see

For more on people or events referred to in this chapter—

I: Found—A Way to See

- Linda Barry: https://drawnandquarterly.com/author/lynda-barry/

- MariNaomi and *I Thought You Loved Me*: https://marinaomi.com

- Maira Kalman and *The Principles of Uncertainty* and *And The Pursuit of Happiness*: https://mairakalman.com/adult and https://www.thecjm.org/exhibitions/24

- Williams, William Carlos. "The Red Wheelbarrow," https://poets.org/poem/red-wheelbarrow

- Edwards, Betty, (1979) *Drawing on the Right Side of the Brain*, Penguin Putnam https://www.drawright.com/bettys-books

- For more about Elliott Coleman: http://fortnightlyreview.co.uk/elliott-colemans-seminary/

- The Writing Seminars at Johns Hopkins: https://writingseminars.jhu.edu/about/history-of-the-department/

I also inquired into image, seeing and art as offering: in Shearer, Cindy, (2018) "The Art of Image: Seeing the Way Home," in M. Garbutt & N. Roenpagel (Eds) & A. Rourke and V. Rees (Series Curators), *The mindful Eye: Contemplative Pedagogies in Visual Arts Education. Transformative Pedagogies in the Visual Domain: Book No. 3.* Champaign, IL: Common Ground Research Networks.

II: Drastic Recounting: A Triptych of Loss and Not Found

Google Maps: Oxford Station, Park End St, Oxford OX1 1HS, United Kingdom to Chilton House, Chilton, Aylesbury HP18 9LR, UK
https://maps.app.goo.gl/1xm7P3duQoaUC16s7
Dick Clark's New Year's Rockin' Eve 1979
https://www.smithsonianmag.com/history/why-do-we-count-down-to-the-new-year-180979289/
Stonewall Uprising
https://guides.loc.gov/lgbtq-studies/stonewall-era
AIDS
https://www.cdc.gov/museum/online/story-of-cdc/aids/index.html

III: Found: Imagining

"Understanding Historic Parks and Gardens in Buckinghamshire." The Buckinghamshire Gardens Trust Research & Recording Project, https://bucksgardenstrust.org.uk/wp-content/uploads/2019/01/Chilton_House.pdf

IV: Found and Loss, Not Quite Found

Tim Gosling https://www.tgosling.com/about/
Soane Museum: https://www.soane.org/about/our-history
Soanian yellow (Soane Yellow SC429). Sample at https://www.farrowball.com/us/paint/dayroom-yellow?finish=full-gloss
Obata, Chiura, (2018), *An American Modern.* Art, Design & Architecture Museum, University of California.
St. Clair, Kassia. *The Secret Lives of Color,* Penguin Books, 2016, 74–6, 78–9.
Hartmann, Elizabeth Anne, "The Most Modern 18th-Century Room You've Ever Seen," Post by *Wall Street Journal,* Feb. 25, 2016, https://www.wsj.com/articles/the-most-modern-18th-century-room-youve-ever-seen-1456423326

Reflection and Exercises

From Elliott, I learned to focus on seeing, to let seeing lead me as I write. What I found for myself is this: If I write what I see as accurately as I can and am curious about, playful with, and probe what I see a bit, I can connect with what I really want to say in my writing—to what matters to me. I try to model that process throughout this book.

I often start writing by seeing an image or something I remember or imagine. Seeing lets me start with someone specific, but underneath what I see is often a question. In this chapter I had two:

1 What story did I want to tell about Elliott and how much of it should I or could I tell?

I realized that to understand the story I wanted to tell, I also needed to understand my capacity—what was I able or willing to write? Two pieces here, "Beautiful Brevities" and "Yellow Room," were already written; they felt like part of the story. I wanted to draft this chapter from multiple perspectives and via the poems— and let my seeing take it from there. I re-worked or revised all the pieces. To create a relationship between the loss I felt and what I found in Elliott, I felt I needed to tell a fuller story. Each essay is (or continues to be) its own piece and offers a story. Relationally, the pieces within the chapter offer another. I also wanted you to see that.

2 How did previously written work shape my memory—and therefore my perspective? How should I work with that?

I realized as I worked on some sections what I could see was via what my previous writing told me I saw. I wanted to test the accuracy of that, so I probed images, events, actions in the new writing (for example, Antioch's financial troubles, Chilton, overhearing), I began to see/remember more things. I wondered—Was I seeing what happened? Or did my feeling about what I remembered influence what I could see now? What I have written feels accurate to me—and I think it is what happened. Some of it I just can't document beyond what I recollect. The chapter integrates what I see now and remember and an interplay between words and form, voice and vantage point, sense details and ideas. These set the boundaries of how I write and what I say.

These essays also subtly offer understandings, or what I have sometimes called awareness or tools. A few include—Seeing, Seeing into, Seeing what matters—and

- Every word counts.

- The writing supports and speaks for itself.

- How we bring ourselves to our work reflects our choices. We determine what we say, what we include, how much we reveal or share.

I'll introduce you to more tools in the chapters ahead and how I developed a "toolbox" of them in Chapter 2.

In Your Journal

Which of the understandings/tools listed above resonate with you? Please list them and stay aware of them as you write. Also, as you reflect on this chapter, what stands out for you? Please reflect on and note that. What questions are provoked in you or what understandings are offered to you? Please record these too and stay aware of them as you write.

Getting to Know Yourself as Writer: Three Exercises

Exercise One: Seeing (Parts 1–3, 30 minutes)

From Elliott, I learned seeing, seeing into, and seeing what matters. I show you how I learned this by stepping inside his writing process—and observing how he wrote and revised his work. I'd like to invite you to also step inside your writing process.

You'll need some index cards or other blank cards (or blank paper cut into small "cards") and a pencil or pen for this exercise. You can write or draw or write and draw, whatever you prefer. If you use blank paper, a pair of scissors will be useful.

Part One: Listing Images (10 minutes)

- Clear your mind. Then step into a time—a summer, a year, a month, a holiday season—that you are willing to explore more. Begin by making a list.

- Make the list quickly. Then pick one time from the list to work with.

- Take your index card or blank paper and make it into "cards." On each card, describe a moment from this time. Focus on the images that arise. See them and describe them in phrases or a sentence or two. Use enough words so you can begin to see the moment clearly in your mind. Or write and draw if this helps you see the images.

Part Two: Seeing Your Images in Relationship to Each Other (10 minutes)

- Read over the cards. Read them aloud so you can really hear them or focus on what you see in the descriptions. Ask yourself—What do these images tell me about this moment? What do they ask me to see? What does each tell me about why this experience matters to me?

- Add to or change your descriptions or images based on your reflections. If a new image arises, create a new card. Describe it or draw it.

- Review all the written or drawn images you have. Begin to arrange them. How do they fit together? Do they all belong, or do you need to edit some out? Keep arranging and editing until you have just the right number to convey what that moment in time is for you.

Part Three: Follow the Images—and Give Your Work Form (10 minutes)

- Construct your piece. Like Elliott, let your list of images guide you, focusing on what to include and what to leave out. Hone your language and create your work. Make a poem or use the "arrangement" of your images as the beginning of a story and let them guide you in the structure of the work. Or use your list of images as a catalyst to draw more and bring text and image together in panels as visual poetry or story.

- Reflect on your piece and what this exercise allowed you to see—and see into your experience. What are you learning about the images that are the core of this experience—and the piece you are creating? What do you learn about yourself as writer and what you are writing?

Next step: Continue to flesh this piece out. Keep working on it, asking What do I see? Draw on or apply relevant tools from this chapter or the remaining chapters to continue to construct this piece.

Exercise Two: Telling Stories: Drastic Recounting (30–35 minutes)

- Reflect on and pick a moment in your life or a fictional moment you'd like to probe more, maybe one like Elliott's that you've held back or kept secret. Would you be willing to offer a drastic recounting of it? (2 minutes).

- Write the moment, tell the story. Consider when the story happens and where (What cultures influence your experience?). Use the present tense (5–7 minutes).

- Read over the story. Circle images that stand out for you, that seem essential to the story. What feels immediate to you? What feels drastic? Note images that feel important and/or that you feel resistant to or uncomfortable with. Ask yourself if you feel able to work with one of them. Pick one image; draw it or visualize it and write it. See it in the moment as clearly as you can (5–7 minutes).

- Review your drawing and/or what you've written. What does it show you? Use that image as your starting point and tell the story again (5–7 minutes).

- Read the story; review what you've written. What is revealed? What questions are there for you? In the image? In the story? In what is missing? In what is unknown? In what you imagine? (5–7 minutes).

- Please reflect on this—What questions in your story are questions for you as artist? (3–5 minutes).

Next step: Review what you've created and your responses to the questions offered. Do you need to sit with it or research it more? If so, give it more time. If you are ready to work more on this, create the story you want others to hear—and list your intended audience.

Exercise Three: Imagining (Seeing Beyond, 35 minutes)

When I wrote about Elliott's poem "Chilton," I saw how "overhearing" helped him to see beyond his experience and imagine the story he wanted to tell. What does imagining allow you to see beyond your experience? In this exercise, you'll create one piece, like "Chilton," with three parts.

- Reflect on places where you've had experiences that stand out for you. Pick one place and the moment in your life or experience or event that happened there. (Feel free to use a place you listed in one of the exercises above.) Write about it in the present tense (5–8 minutes).

- Review what you've written and pick something (a memory, image, or conversation) you wish was different or you could change. Focus on it. Maybe overhear it. What questions are underneath your desire to alter or shift the experience? Write the questions and let them shape this section of the piece (5–8 minutes).

- Review what you've created so far. What speaks to you? What's missing from the experience or what would you add to your experience? Visualize this and/or draw it, so you can really see it. Once you can see this, use it to imagine the story. Write that version. What emerges?

Next steps: Bring the present-tense story, the question-driven version, and the imagined story together in one piece or focus on developing the imagined story. What are you aware of as you write? What are the choices you make?

Integrative Exercise

Review all you've created here: What stands out for you? What are you learning about your writing? Yourself as writer? List what you've enjoyed and are curious to work with more.

2 WHY I QUIT WRITING AND HOW I FOUND A NEW ART FORM

My brother visits. I tell him there are some photographs in a storage chest, a scrapbook my mother had. We agree to look at them. Sunday afternoon, we do. I give him the scrapbook—he realizes it is very personal—he finds photos of friends, a valentine from a man my mother knew years before she married our father. He wonders if looking through these private documents of hers is okay.

I find an envelope filled with things that I have not looked through in the thirty-six years she has been dead. There is a long letter—an epistle, she calls it, of a trip to Florida she took in 1951 with some female friends. I assume she wrote it and don't know who she sent it to (I'm guessing one of her sisters). It has the feel of a letter to someone, not just a record, a way of documenting her experience. It is on tracing paper, the kind we used when we made carbon copies while typing. There is no Dear _____ or name or signature at the end; she doesn't identify herself as the writer.

There are also four letters I sent to her or her and my father from London in 1978. I did not know she kept these. Why these four? There would have been many more. I wrote her frequently. In one, I told her Elliott was "beginning to lose his ability to discern reality," and wonder who talks like that. I don't remember sharing that idea—or believing it. I go on to worry it is possible someone working at Chilton was not treating him well. Again, I have no memory of this or of saying that. I am surprised by and unsure of this person with such clear views—so young, but so informed. "It is sad sometimes to think of being old. What loneliness. I don't know." I am struck how memory holds what it holds, not necessarily truth—and I feel cautious stepping into the remembering I am doing now. I am surprised in general by how much I say in the letter. I remember being cautious. My memory is that I kept a lot to myself.

There is a passbook for a small savings account, the last deposit September 20, 1976, a letter from May 1968 that my mother's sister Betty Jo sent (King's Daughter's Hospital School of Nursing as the return address) explaining what polymorphous light sensitive eruption is, a condition my mother developed after she was burned in a kitchen fire, and a pamphlet on Lupus Erythematosus, a later diagnosis. There is also a certificate from the Vacation Bible School of Central Baptist Church in recognition of her "faithful attendance and credible work" in summer 1938, a typed, not printed article, "The ABC's of Guiding the Child" by Rudolf Dreikurs, MD (it is on its own—no envelope or label), and her signature, Mrs. Robert Shearer, on the back of my sister's report card, 1960–61. A letter from Social Security states she'll need thirty-three quarters of "coverage" to qualify for benefits. In 1974, she has thirty-two.

There is also a poem I believe I wrote in 1978. I've typed my name at the bottom of the A4 sheet and signed the poem with my first name, but there is no date. The A-4 is folded lengthwise four times; it is trace-paper thin. But the paper is wider than the small envelopes I used to send letters, so the folded notepaper would not fit inside. The letters in small envelopes cost 20p to send; there is one 11p and one 9p stamp on them and the small blue sticker: by airmail par avion. The blue airmail letters, also trace-paper thin, cost 10½p to send. I had to fold and seal them; it wasn't possible to slip anything inside them. My handwriting is small but exact.

There is nothing in the large manila envelope to suggest that the poem was included in a letter, sent on its own, or maybe just given to her. It is just there among everything else. That doesn't mean much—so much has been moved and placed and replaced since her death. There was everyone going through things to decide what they wanted and then the packing and unpacking during my move from Ohio to California. Later, there was my move from one house to another, and, of course, there are all the times we've been through the cabinet looking for other things and it wasn't like we carefully put everything back where we found it. It hasn't been that kind of life.

It was not like me to share my work with them. A lot of reasons for that. Yet I had sent this one. I had given it to them. I don't reference it or say why.

My brother works away on the scrapbook—reading captions out loud. He is fifty-five years older than he was in the small photograph that is the

reference point for the poem, but in a weird way, if we stood together in a
park again, we'd look like the well-worn siblings we are, our childhood
affinity for each other still visible. I'm sure I would not wear a bathing suit
but my brother might.

Photograph

beach
state park

        Whitewater
        Indiana

brother
hair cropped
swimming trunks

           sister
           pixie   short bangs
           two-piece bathing suit

each
    one arm over the other's shoulder

    polaroid
        still that pose

black
   white
      1965

In my work from that era, there is always so much of what is not said,
as well as what is, a negative space, a focus on the images to invite us to
see, to ask what is also there. From Elliott, I learned if we see first, then we
can also glimpse what is available to us underneath or inside it. I learned
if I focus on what I can with my eyes or inside my mind, my seeing can
unearth or lead me to what I want or need to say.

I wouldn't write poems like it now. I don't write poetry now. The poem
is part of an earlier time in my life and imagist history. I would, however,

still strive for simplicity. I'm still interested in the meaning one visual word can have—and the complexity one word in relationship to another can have. Now, even more, I focus on seeing.

I include this poem here because it says something about what I valued early in my writing life and because I returned to what this writing offered me when later I lost my work or gave it up. When I needed to remake myself, I looked back at what had been—and used that as a place to start from and eventually to revise, maybe reinvent myself. I say I quit writing because I did not do it for a long time—but really, in many ways, I was lost, more like at a loss, and I had to re-find myself and the work.

The poem is my brother and me; the photograph is from the first scrapbook I made once I got my own camera. The poem reminds me of the tenderness I have had for my brother, that I had for the visual (while living in London) and language (each word). I can see the influence of seeing, the beautiful brevities. Later, when I quit writing, I'll cut it up and make it into something else—and it will be part of the process for me of finding my way back to my work.

*　*　*

I don't make what I am supposed to. I don't make anything.

Sometime in the early 1990s, I just quit writing. I don't remember deciding that. I just didn't do it. I didn't want to do it, didn't feel like it. I want to say I didn't have anything to say—but that is just a feeling that comes up. I still wanted to be a writer, but I didn't want to write. I knew from Elliott that writers write, and I didn't. I didn't care about it—I didn't believe in it. I don't remember ever really recognizing the decision I'd made; it's just something that I did, meaning that I didn't do, until I'd committed to creating a personal essay for a conference and realized I didn't write any more.

Time collapses in my memory here, but in a space of years, my mother died, I gave birth, I was raising a young child with a marriage imploding—on my way to, or in the midst of, divorce—I'd had many, many rejections of my work—and few acceptances. I'd walked away from a full-time teaching position in which I felt very boxed in. I'd acquired some skills/training in documentary video/film and my husband—soon to be ex-husband—was supposed to help co-create but, like much else in the relationship, partnership in every form was deteriorating. I could detail the list of things that picked away at my interest in language and desire to write—but in the end, it was all the above and one cold fact—I didn't care about it. It did not feel meaningful to me. A writer was someone I wanted to be—and the disconnect between that and actually writing was vast, the leap between what I wanted and/or hoped for was more than I could navigate. My writing felt dead—and yet I had committed and could not deliver. I had no idea why, let alone what to do, except watch the deadline get closer and the chances of me meeting it farther away.

Everything has an origin story, and for me, I wonder if the story begins in this image:

I was twelve, at home with my mother, eating breakfast. I started school late in the day. Our junior high school was overcrowded, so, eighth grade went in the morning, seventh grade (my year) in the afternoon. The district was building a new school, not ready yet, and the old one didn't have room for all of us. The solution was split school days.

Everyone else was gone—my father to work, my sister in high school and brother in elementary. My mother was in robe and nightgown. I was dressed, finishing my toast. She was standing by the dishwasher. The robe was green, not expensive, more Sears than Elder-Beerman. I can see the green collar, beaded or embroidered, sewn on like a patch, not into the fabric. I could tell she wanted to place a fork in the dishwasher, but her body wouldn't respond. She was reaching out and a fork was dangling from her hand, but it seemed not to want to release it. I can see the green robe unbuttoned, open, the nightgown to her knees thin offering a hint of flesh underneath. She must have worn slippers, she was not a barefoot kind of person, but I can't see them. I see the same square body, same round waist, the chunky arms and legs I also have, and the sleeve of the robe ¾ length, a hand outstretched. Does she know something is off? There was a lag, a disconnect in everything she did. I looked up and she was talking (or trying to), but her mouth looked to be heading one direction and the words another. Everything was out of sync.

I called my father. He came home from work. My mother went to the doctor—stroke was mentioned but not explained—so I just waited. I knew what stroke meant—my grandmother, paralyzed on her left side, had had one years before and was currently residing in Kentucky stationed in a high-back, rose-colored chair with embroidered footstool. There wasn't if my mother would have another stroke, but when. The not talking about it meant it was mine to carry, to watch and wait for. At that moment, I did not literally have to care for my mother, but I think it became the moment in which I cared and knew the responsibility inherent in that would call on me.

I understood the fabric of life, like her nightgown, was thin—it splits easily, that there is fragility within every moment and every life, but I separated from that insight, resisting it as best I could.

Eighteen years later, in 1988, my mother had that next stroke—the first of many. The moment for care arrived. Maybe I'd waited (a kind of training?) my whole life to care for her.

For me, I think what ultimately broke my writing process was my mother's death—I'd struggled after Elliott's death—the doctorate was difficult for me, since Elliott died my first year in coursework. I completed the degree, but never really settled in, I felt untethered personally and professionally—and my lack of success was on my mind—fiction written, fiction rejected. Failure, loss, failure, failure, failure. The details blend; I'm not sure which matter most. The reality is—I could not make much happen with the work—and my life was not in a place to support me in finding my way—and I did not have belief. I lost belief in myself.

The surgeon said he would not take on a blockage at the base my mother's neck, so like the uncertainty of what would happen next, it just sat there, soundlessly like a clock winding down. We didn't talk about this; it was just one of the things reported to me. We never knew how many strokes she had. All we knew was she was being chipped away—one part of her body at a time. After the first stroke and even the second, the doctors talked about rehabilitation and how she could learn to walk again. Then, there was no more talk like that. Instead, she was drifting more and more silently toward death and away from us.

For months I largely gave myself to caring for my mother along with a beloved home-health aide, a hospice nurse, my father, brother, sister, aunts, and then-husband. He and I uprooted ourselves from another state, moving into her and my father's home. My world was contained and repetitious. My mother had to be fed, exercised, bathed. There was laundry and dirty dishes. I'd grind or mash food as swallowing became more and more difficult for her. I'd get up in the middle of the night and take the stairs down to her room, which was actually the family room, now with a hospital bed instead of a couch, to make sure she was breathing. In the morning, the chores started again.

Though occasionally I kept some notes in a journal, I forgot about fiction and creative non-fiction—they felt totally irrelevant to me.

Between the caretaking and the fluctuating emotions circulating through the house, there was quiet. In stillness, the message I heard was you don't need to create. The message from publishers, "not for us," I heard as the work is not good enough. The message from me—who cares?

Then my mother died, the mother who sat with me after Elliott died, who understood the depression we called being tired. I had been waiting for her death. For much of my life, I'd been waiting for the stroke to come. She had been the center of our family—without her—it did not take long for the holes in the rest of my life to become highly visible, what was collapsing sharply evident.

I was accumulating loss personally, holding rejection/failure professionally. I shut down; I quit writing. I had writing in files instead of work out to literary journals or agents or small presses. I had fiction in drawers, essays started, maybe completed, short stories, poems (a first teacher) that I'd put away.

One of the last photographs my ex-husband took of my mother and I before her stroke is the two of us sitting on the living room couch together. Someone has given me a perm—and my hair, puffy and frizzy at the same time, looks 1987 ridiculous. Despite that, I have my arm over her shoulder, and I lean my head against her. It's a reminder relationship is so much more than what is said.

My aunt said that soon after her father died, she heard a trumpet sounding in the night, and when she awakened, she saw a white spirit in the room. She believes the spirt was her father saying good-bye. Many people, I know, have similar experiences.

I have never felt my mother once. I don't know where she is. I have lost her. The feeling I struggled with was that, because I lost her, I was also losing some of myself. I also felt this way when I lost Elliott.

In writing, I had the experience of turning events, observations, insights into something beautiful in words. I'd experimented, experimented, experimented, testing what words could do, but I lost the discipline, the will for writing practice. Like my life, the writing got more distant. When my mother became ill, and it was clear she would die, my practice lost its life too.

It would be more than fifteen years before writing would be the primary focus of my work again. I did find my way back to my writer's life; along the way, I learned finding sustainability, a way and reason to stay with it (more than a narrow view of success) is key to writing well-being for me.

I. Finding a Form: Postcards

I had an immediate problem. I'd agreed to write a piece—a personal essay/memoir—and present at conference—and I just couldn't do it.

I literally had nothing to say—but I did have a colleague who was a visual artist—and he'd invited students to draw. That intrigued me. I read Pat B. Allen's *Art is a Way of Knowing* and Betty Edwards's *Drawing on the Right Side of the Brain* and tried drawing myself: focusing on the lines, on what they allowed me to capture and see, but for me, the path to drawing was internal image—one to capture from inside my mind. If I allowed image to arise in my mind, if I could see it, what did it invite me to draw?

I drew two chairs. I remember the two chairs were facing each other, as if in conversation; again, memory seems to see what it wants to see. When I looked at the drawing recently, one chair is behind the other— one chair is leading? The other following? Or are they in a line moving forward together? They are close, they might even be touching but only one can see the other.

Yet creating them seemed to be enough—because once I started drawing the chairs, they just kept on coming—then their shapes changed—female, male, like ghosts or dancers, dressed in bright colors or leaping in flight. I started therapy. I made more work. I shared the work with the therapist, but the artmaking was mine and it began to morph. At a conference, I presented a tentative piece suggesting drawing could be of value for writers.

I made more drawings and then drawing became postcards as shown in Figure 2.

On the back is the text. Later, I made a handmade stamp (a green square with red flame, 20 USA, for twenty cents) for it.

"1/12/98

This is my mother's grave. Her body waits under the ground. It is naked, still pink, aware of the forces of life all around. She doesn't have a head anymore—can't know or speak. What we want to tell her is too late to say. Instead of words, there is flame."

The process was simple. I saw, I drew, I let image lead me. When I finished the drawing, I turned the card over and wrote, maybe in response to the image, maybe in conversation with it, maybe to clarify the relationship between what I drew and what I had to say, often to speak to

FIGURE 2 *This is My Mother's Grave*, Postcard, 5" x 7", 1998. Watercolor paper and oil pastel

the person I was writing to. Each card was addressed to someone. I think the actual speaking to someone was important—I delivered the cards as gifts. For me, the gifting was important. It was a way of going beyond myself—of making, even forcing, an audience for the work.

Communicating (via what was shown and said) was motivating. Each card also had a stamp—a hand-made stamp, a stamp of declaration, sometimes surety. It was literally a stamp, something drawn or glued onto the card. For me, the stamp was the visual bridge between the text and the image. It connected them or it brought out one or more elements of the scene or story.

What began to interest me the most was that I was making an object. I was making art that included words. It had an aesthetic core—I was letting it originate and then develop and become itself—a fully realized object—I could do this—it was fun and provoking in unexpected ways. Eventually I'd realize there was much I could take from this to writing—and I would reimagine the process.

Fun fact: The word postcard comes from the word "post" meaning, to put, place. Creating a postcard for me was about discovering that I wanted to place something and was making a place for it. I valued the discovery of postcards as the process of placing.

Later, I developed a set of *Ten Not-so-Tangible Tools for Writers* as support for someone who was writing a first book. I made a text/image book on writing and offered it to him (and later included it in an art show). The irony is not lost on me; I had quit writing but was creating a book about writing. The work was a gift, maybe more like an act of giving; again, I thought of it as a way to engage someone, to tangibly have a reader, to support another's writing, since I couldn't support my own. The book was about writing but using text/image as form, so it was also artmaking—a way of placing writing with art.

"But this book talks more about the not-so-tangible tools, what I think of as 'precepts of awareness,' that writers can benefit from and need. I believe these precepts and have created this book as a model of how we can use ways of being aware as writing tools. Using these precepts of awareness can affect what and how we write. They can offer us a new approach or a different attitude and can help us develop our writing practice. They invite us to be curious. They allow us to stretch and bend. They remind us not to get discouraged and help us pay attention to what's really important . . .

"What are the tools that writers need? Tangible and not-so-tangible tools,"

Ten Not-so-Tangible Tools for Writers, mixed media, 2001

I like the word *tool*, as, years ago, I was playing with tools being something we could hold or use, whether we could literally hold them or not. Now, all these years later, I like reflecting on the tools as understandings, in addition to awarenesses. Understanding for me allows for care and kindness, and it suggests agreement or something I have belief in. I like the vibe of the word—and that even as we work with an understanding, we can continue to be curious about it, so it can be altered or continue to grow and change. I think of the tools/understandings as a meditation on what's possible in the relationship between text/image, between maker and making, writer and writing. I focus on two tools here (writing is mending and writing is relationship), and one I've developed more recently (writing is offering).

Writing is Mending

When I say mending, I can see a physical act of repair—needle and thread stitching a well-worn garment, each act of sewing a part of putting together what has been pulled apart. When we mend, either by writing or sewing, our stitches stay. Whether they are easy to see or hidden within our fabric, they remain.

Maybe we are always mending, whatever the intention or the form of our writing. Maybe we are always putting back together what has been pulled apart. I wonder if whenever we write deeply, we aren't desiring to mend. One way to uncover what we are mending is by noticing the repetitions that occur in our work. Sometimes we convey our need to mend through subjects we write about again and again. Sometimes we repeat words or images. Sometimes certain stories, anecdotes, or descriptions frequently recur.

But how does writing help us mend? When it allows us to uncover new layers of meaning and experience or to discover much that we were not aware of before? When it allows us to construct a tangible object, one that we can examine, share with another, hold? Yes and yes. But there is more. When we mend through writing, we sew ourselves back together. We make the repair. Our writing tells us we are mending. Look. The stitches are there.

"Writing is Mending," *Ten-Not-So Tangible Tools for Writers*,
mixed media, 2001

Early on, I did a lot of mending in the postcards. For writing is mending, I created an image of a female body. She has space rather than a head, a thread and needle making stitches through what is likely a heart. The images rests on glossy paper, the kind we use to wrap a gift.

For me, mending was a first understanding, important because I needed to know it was possible. I needed to recognize I could mend before I could move forward.

I often tell writers that writing/artmaking is inherently a reparative process. I think even if a writer doesn't want their work to focus on that, there is comfort in knowing it can.

A piece that had long been missing began to fall into place for me; to create, I had to have something to say—and I needed to see how to say it. I began to see that the relationship between what to say and how to say it could be different for every work.

What I began to call writing as art originated in drawing—but, as I say above, it quickly became postcards and more. What I was exploring in postcards was how image could be a catalyst or in dialogue or conversation with the writing—and then, the most important thing, the stamp—what was needed to share the work (to mail a postcard, it must have a stamp), but also the stamp is what allows it to be in relationship, a communication, from the maker to someone else. The idea of writing as relationship became fundamental to me.

I began to see the postcard as the perfect art form (text, image, stamp).

There was value for me in making a new form—one that felt like art as I wanted to define it—it helped me to see much about what was possible in words. I was making all kinds of things, but I was always thinking about what I was saying—and how I could give more heft, more dimension to words. It was also teaching me the value of other arts—and what they could bring to writers.

II. In Relationship and A Puzzle

On the outside, another poem—

between autumns

autumn again

        no leaves
on my tree

only trunk
      branch
      bark
root

September
red and yellow

against
the green grass

this
        is Independence

just another
season

brittle
by November

          I have seen before

Looking now at this piece after so many years, the colors surprise me. They are not obviously autumn colors; they contrast with the words. There is the poem and a door to open, inside are layers of photographs with text and image. One has to pull them back to get all the way inside. On the other side of the puzzle is the photo of my brother and me, and my poem layered within it (the one from the beginning of this chapter).

FIGURE 3 *Puzzle*, 5" x 7", 1998.
Text, oil pastels, photographs, puzzle pieces

Or, another way to say it, the puzzle has two sides, one always visible and one always unseen (or hidden). In the spirit of relationship, the two sides of the card exist together—but one can only view them separately. Yet, once seen, the viewer can create a relationship between them.

The words and photographs also cover the spaces where the puzzle pieces fit together so the work cannot be taken apart but gives the illusion it could be.

As an artist, I trained first as a poet – and though I work in other forms now, I try to bring a poetic sensibility to all that I create. The work I make arises from the word—it builds from the individual word and in relationship to other words within the piece. Words ask me to see—and from that seeing—what they suggest or evoke matters to me—and I often construct my work from what the words offer me. In text and image work that often means weaving words into visual frames. The visual object offers a way into or can be a companion to the experience or the story the language shares. Over time, I'd use my understanding of all this to reach for the visual capacity of words in storytelling.

In my exhibit Writing as Art (2003), my artist statement said (in part):

I seek connection through art making.
I am making relationships when I work.

Writing as Art, on the surface, allows me to create connection between text and image. More deeply, it allows me layers of relationships—with what I want to say, with those I am speaking to, with the form my work takes. In artmaking, I am in a continuing conversation on the importance of connection and our strong need to mend disconnection, on the simplicity and mystery of relationship, and on ways that genuine engagement with beauty can restore and sustain us.

I defined writing as art as a way of "reconfiguring the boundaries of writing and visual art and of finding ways of bringing text and image together: I have joined tangible materials with the writing process. I have constructed visual work as I would a written text." In "Intention," in *And Then, You Act: Making Art in an Unpredictable World*," Anne Bogart writes, "What are you doing? What are you tempting?" sharing that intention is in relationship with our choices about what we make and why (2007, 35). For me, it is a way of mapping all we commit to in the artmaking and the art. From approximately 1996–2011, I made postcards including postcards with "pop-outs" and three dimensions, maps, self-portraits, many stories in boxes and on hardboards, and *Ten Not-So-Tangible Tools for Writers*, a book in text and image and a toolbox.

In my artist statement, I also shared my practices and how they engaged what I care about, another way of naming intention:

- By connecting with my female sensibility and creating relationship with a woman's world. I've valued the personal and relational as ways to engage the core, essential, and universal inside us.

- By creating relationship with the life I live. As a single parent, I've made much of this work on my dining room table and constructed it in brief, often interrupted, periods of time.

- By bringing together the everyday with the exotic—simple art materials (such as card stock and oil pastels), flowers and leaves from my backyard with Tibetan silver, Australian crystal beads, black pearls from Hawaii. I've come to believe pleasure derives from joining the mundane and the real, the mysterious and the fictional, the actual and the fantasized.

Though I was working with visual materials, writing as art helped me see words again, see them for what they can say, see them for what's possible with them, see them for the relationship they can generate.

Writing is relationship

Actually, it's two relationships. Well, maybe, it's three.

Relationship #1: When you write, you are in relationship with yourself. Think of you and your text as having a self-to-self conversation. It's a dialogue that lets you get at the essence of your experience and discover what you want to say.

Relationship #2: You are in relationship with a reader. As you write, you talk with and to a reader. Maybe it's a reader you know well or one you can clearly imagine. Maybe it's a reader you aren't so sure of or can't clearly see. Whether you are comfortable or not, the reader is there. Feel the presence. Feel into the experience. Feel what you feel. Just don't forget to relate.

Relationship #3: Readers have a relationship with you. If they're interested in what you say, they'll stay connected. If not, they'll be gone. It's all about the quality of relationship you have with them and you let them have with you. It's really up to you.

So listen. Pay attention. Take care of these relationships as you would any other. When you speak well to yourself, you will likely speak well to your reader. When you are responsive to your reader, your reader will likely respond to you. Treated well by your reader, you will probably take care of yourself. One relationship feeds another. Say what you think. Say what you want. Be authentic. Be yourself. Consider what the other needs and wants. Find your optimal distance. Find your optimal intimacy.

Then, have a seat at the keyboard, take your shoes off, type away. Enjoy yourself. You are connected. You are in relationship. You are not alone.

"Writing is Relationship,"
Ten-Not-So Tangible Tools for Writers, mixed media, 2001

My text/image work, including *Puzzle* (above), often involved cutting up what was already made and making it new—I did that again and again. I wanted to include *Puzzle* here because it started out a poem and then became a puzzle, or represented a puzzle, since the pieces were set. It was the beginning of my understanding that in artmaking I constructed relationship—I made something that I connected with and wanted others to connect with also. In *Puzzle*, and many other pieces, I was learning to play in relationship with the tangible and intangible in artmaking. From *Puzzle*, I learned the following:

- The two poems I brought together in the piece did not have to directly relate; they could simply be in relationship to each other and influence how viewers and I related to the work.

- The materials (the puzzle, poems, photos, drawing, color) in relationship to each other allowed for building relationships between the text and visual elements—and interrelationships among the materials in the piece. Relationship, I began to see, provided structures for more relationship.

- By linking past and present, pairing what I remembered with my insights and understandings now, the loss of relationship with the claiming of relationship, I could relate what was or what happened to what something can become when it is remade or reimagined.

In this work and others like it, I began to ask myself—What can be created? What is and what can be evoked? In sharing this work, I want to show how it encouraged, even required, a willingness to play—a dedicated play that allowed for artmaking that was inter-relational and valued relationship. It sometimes led to good work and sometimes led to more learning. For me, both are important. What I would ultimately bring to writing is the understanding that multiple ways of relating are always present whether in the creating of work or in the experience of it—and I wanted to be conscious of and attentive to all of them.

I didn't allow for this in the work that I created earlier in my life. I didn't allow that there was more than one relationship or route possible— all work began, was written and revised (likely numerous times) and was sent to the world (for publication or presentation or some other acknowledgment), whether it was ready or not. I was learning that making art/writing asks for dialogue—with materials, ways of engaging and possible meanings, and choices about how to work with and use them.

I worked for long time with various forms, each giving me more space and skills for telling stories, either via text and image or through words. Each was part of the process of returning to my writing self and writing. I could write again and be a writer again. I learned I had to move through my process entirely, all the way through the process, to make realized work. I was a writer but being a writer was becoming something different for me. It was first asking questions and staying with them—letting what was unknown, not realized, uncertain but what wanted and needed to be known drive the work—and trusting the process of following all that. It was okay to be curious; it was okay to care and use those things as a foundation for the work. I learned that claiming what I value—what I care about and am willing to work for—is at the core of successfully constructing and sustaining my work.

The experience of loss, of losing my writing, was in part tied to things that happened—two important deaths or other life events, for sure, but it was also decisions I made, what I was not aware of or didn't see, choices I could envision or not. What I missed in the first version of myself as writer was not asking what happened when I compromised my vision. I did not ask—Did it work? Did the parts sing? Work together? Was the work ready for public view, let alone, publishing? If I sat alongside my process, instead of in relationship to it, could the work ever work?

I took a circuitous route—making my own form so I could re-find existing forms. I needed to do that so I could find a process that I could also apply to working with them. I think we all need to find what works for us. That's why I talk about writing as a set of choices; I think we need to know what questions to ask, what decisions to make for ourselves and our work.

What I did not want again was to disconnect from audience or let the vagaries of publishing dull my care for my work. What I've learned from my years of writing and working with writers to publish their work in myriad forms is that we often push to publish too soon. We push before the work is ready. I learned we need to recognize for ourselves when it is—and be ready to weather the process, however it turns out. If we don't, we can lose heart if it fails. It can keep us from writing.

I can return to writing as art as a focus for my work whenever I want to. But the tools, experiences, and understandings I have from it, I draw on every day in my writing.

III. Offering (and Green Tara): Where are You?

A few years after I created my ten tools, I began to reflect on the word *offering* and how in writing/artmaking we take in what is offered to us and use it to make our work, offering back what we've made. I think of offering as what we have to give. We offer for ourselves (for our own reasons) and to something beyond us—other people, causes, organizations, groups. I see offering as an act, how we offer, and an offering, the thing we offer. I explored this in an exhibit I curated, *Offering: Works of Text and Image* (2011).

From this exhibit and the writing/art I was making at the time, I began to understand two additional things: (1) Learning from my writing/art was important to me; by engaging in artmaking, I was offering to learn from it, and (2) I could not predict outcome: Would I be able to publish what I created? Find an exhibit for it? I hoped so (and would skillfully try to do that)—but I'd offer it anyway.

Early on in my writing as art practice, as I mentioned earlier, I focused on art as gift, as choosing to give. Later, I realized gift-giving is fraught in certain ways. You give a gift and someone has to take it—who says (or feels able to say) they don't want or would not like to have the gift. And, if the gift is unwelcome or refused, that can be hurtful to the giver. Gifting, I realized, begins as a generous act—but really it can be complicated for the giver and the receiver—and the idea of "giving away" carries a lot of

FIGURE 4 *Green Tara, Where are You?,* Hardboard 18" x 24", 2004.
Handmade papers, wood box, watercolor paper, stones from Bali, personal journal, dried flowers, brass hinges

connotations, some about the value of the work. There was a freedom in giving to or giving away, but it left me with questions about my responsibility to the work. I realized just as we need to choose our work, readers/viewers need to choose it too.

Offering is offering but it exists in relationship. Once we make our work, once we write something, we can offer it to others, and we don't know what will happen. The offering may or may not be accepted or received. I've learned we may need to make our offerings more than once for them to be taken in or accepted—or we may need to offer them in new, revised or different ways, at a later time, or from a new or altered perspective. The writing/art may not have been fully ready for offering, or culture, place, circumstances may have changed and those not wanting to receive it are more ready for it now, or maybe we have changed and our offering needs to show that. Again, we have to be attentive to relationship—who are we offering to and why? We make, we offer, maybe offer again, the same way or as something new. Offering allows for that. Maybe you've opened a drawer and a work that has been sitting there feels ready for revision—or maybe twenty years have passed, and, as a writer I know has shared, you can finally finish a work started then—and find an agent who is interested in it.

For me, offering provides a satisfying orientation: Is the work ready to be offered? If yes, how to do that? If no, the response can be as important as the work itself: Return to the work and re-see it. Or return to my intentions for the work and keep probing them and the relationship between them. Or let the work rest—it may need more time.

For me, the learning was—offer the work when I was ready and understand that readiness includes being able to accept the consequences of offering. That might be different from the hoped-for success. I've come to understand that if I am ready to make the offering, then I'm inherently ready to accept what happens when I offer it. I'm ready to keep offering, even if that means nothing happens, and I have to wait or reassess. I value the tensions that arise in artmaking—between what I offer and how it is received—and how I choose to relate to the process of offering.

Green Tara: Where Are You? plays with my understanding that offering can be re-offering, creating new art from what I've offered at another time or in a different form. It includes pieces of writing and journal entries I wrote a long time ago (for example, pages from a notebook I kept of visits to the British Library), bits of jewelry and other artifacts from my past, and I make them into something new. I took the journal apart, made it a new size and gave it new binding. I make a connection to the past and reimage it—adding texture, color and a box for offerings and a book to offer a new point of view. I also make a new book of text/image from sturdy black paper and a binding that incorporates beads and stones, and what I wanted to say "right now." The text is simple, repetitive. Green Tara is not there, but that's okay; I give her the form I can. I offer what I have to give.

One of the things I've learned as a writer from making work on hardboards that incorporate three-dimensional elements, such as boxes, is that flat surfaces provide possibilities for textures and structures. In *Green Tara: Where Are You?* and other pieces I made on wood panels, I used textures, layers of paper, fabrics, dried flowers, leaves, rosemary sprigs. As a writer, I think about that now as I use words: What do I want the reader to touch? How tactile can I make the use of words? With boxes—and the things that go inside them, I learned how and where to place structures: I asked, how do I want to call attention to them? I don't think I made perfect choices on this—but I learned that there were good reasons for placing them in an unexpected place or asking the eye to travel to look at them. If the eye has to go to the box or other item, it will look at it. It will note what is there. In my writing, I now think more about structures that interrupt or invite the reader to take in something unexpected. I consider this part of the relationship I am building with them—do I surprise or startle them? As my eye moves around the story or the description or the image, do I invite them to join me—or do I want to use language that asks for or lets them travel on their own? To do these things well, I feel I need clarity on what I am offering them—and the words and structures to form that.

IV. Story Boxes—Imagining

I don't remember how I got interested in boxes or exactly why I decided to construct stories in them, except I liked the physicality of text/image work, that my hands were constructing work. I could build things out of textures and materials and items I could string together or sew. I loved making the characters myself and imaging their stories as I cut out the fabric that shaped them; I wanted not just to imagine what I was creating, I wanted to make it and feel it in my hand.

I loved opening the lid of a box and seeing the world that might be there; I imagined, and maybe like Elliott when he wrote "Chilton," I wanted to show the story unfolding, as I was putting the pieces of it together.

A box, of course, is a simple, everyday thing. Box by box, we let them pile up in our closets or garages, or we break them down and place them in recycling. Most of what we order online comes in a box: Shoe box, hat box, Priority Mail box, box of chocolates or cookies, bankers' box.

I began by using Papier-Mâché boxes because they could hold paint and other materials—and were sturdier than cardboard. I wanted to create/make the characters who lived inside each box—so I began to shape them out of 300-pound watercolor paper, in later boxes, to fashion them out of fabric remnants and sew their bodies together. I made them necklaces or belts, purses or suitcases. I gave them feathers in their hair or sometimes earrings. I was imagining them and the world I wanted to create, so sometimes they were more like symbols, a living mythology.

I realized, of course, a box is also a container. A place to make a story but with only so much room to move. I created a story inside a wood box that had a black metal clasp and hinges on the back. When I pulled up on the clasp and raised the lid, two watercolor-paper characters, painted sky blue with small blue shoulder bags with white straps and red trim, could slide up and down the ridges of a heavy watercolor-paper sky inside the lid. "Sky Box," also had four lidded spaces inside it. Each space was a different environment—wilderness, red rock desert, river, campfire; parts of the story, a pilgrimage, were embedded in the characters' belongings and underneath the lids. The more I worked with boxes the more I realized a box has so much more space than you think—a lid, sides, bottom, top of the lid, underneath the lid, but it is still a defined space. It limits the perspective we can offer. "Sky Box" had multiple spaces but limited space, so I had to reduce the story to its essence, just the moment I wanted viewers to see. It made me ask—What can be contained? What can be left out? The limits helped me shape how I could see and construct the story, a lesson that would also directly carry over into my writing.

I made fourteen boxes in several years—and then over time began to add or incorporate boxes into the hardboards I made, *Green Tara, Where Are You?* and others, such as *Offering* and *Rose Petal Offering.* The boxes added a layer of story, an additional perspective, objects that could be touched, a scroll inside a ring, a Tibetan bell, dried rose petals, kindling wrapped in green ribbon wrapped around a female figure's waist, Green Tara inside a handmade book. What was offered was inside the box—or in the text woven with handmade paper onto the canvas. Viewers, if they wanted, could take in what I was offering them.

When I returned to writing, boxes would stay with me—via how to tell visual stories in a contained way. I was ready to imagine in a new way, not hand-made worlds, but in words. *Haiku Box* (next page), a companion to Sky Box, is the tiniest box I made—it has held that worn feel for more than twenty years. For me, it holds the same simplicity as the poem shared at the beginning of this chapter—a lot can be said in small space, if we are directed to see.

V. Writing is Art, Lost and Found

I didn't realize for a long time that loss—and feeling lost because of it—are inevitable. In *A Field Guide to Getting Lost,* Rebecca Solnit tells us

FIGURE 5 *Haiku Box*, Papier-Mâché Box, 2" x 3", 2001.
Mixed Media, fabric, stones, watercolor paper

nineteenth-century explorers were willing to get lost because they remained optimistic that they would survive and would ultimately find their way (2005, 13–14). For me this applies to every range of experience, including making art. She writes "For it is not, after all, really a question about whether you can know the unknown, arrive in it, but how to go about looking for it, how to travel" (2005, 24).

My understanding continues to evolve, but a core of sustainable practice for me is to travel with curiosity into the unknown, trusting (as nineteenth-century explorers did) that I'll find my way. I can do that by–

1   taking care of the relationships within the work and with those I make it for, first seeing then understanding the impact I want it to have. Others will say what they want it to achieve or what it should be, but I need to define and reach for that myself. Otherwise, I am not making my work and disconnection can kick in.

2   linking meaning to what I care about. I've learned it is important
not to lose sight of what I experience and to be willing to probe it,
no matter where the works takes me. Form is just form if it is not
tied to something I care about. I learned that meaning is best
constructed when the impact I want to have and what I see are in
relationship.

I quit and started again. Quitting was easy, but also painful. Starting
again was hard. Once I quit, I had to ask what reason or what motivation
I had to try again. I learned that when there is loss, to try again, something
has to be found. The found thing for me was writing as art. It made writing
something for me, while it reminded me that I already knew what it was.

Sustainable suggests something that can be maintained at a certain rate
or level and/or something that can be upheld or defended. Sustainable is
often used as an adjective so it also relies on relationship (for example,
sustainable + life, sustainable + practice). The quality of the process
matters—I can ask myself what is my sustainable level? But also I need to
be able to affirm it. When questions come up, doubt sets in, can I rely on it?

Solnit quotes Thoreau saying that to get lost a man has only to close
his eyes and be completely turned around once (2005, 14–15). It can
happen that quickly, and writing as art has taught me, it takes that much
trust.

VI. Works in Progress: Writing in Image

remnant
noun: a remaining
adjective: remaining

The Shoebox Sewing Box
2019

I open the Nike shoebox, the sewing box my mother had before she
died. On the outside is what's left of a label stating, "USA 10 ½," much
too big for my mother, and "Reg $59.95" but marked down to $39.95.
Oddly, inside is a smaller Bass shoebox. In black marker on masking
tape on one side of the box, not in my mother's handwriting, is "Sewing

Box." I don't remember ever having a conversation with her (or anyone) about the box. I remember only that the supplies within it seemed like something I could use, a good thing to keep, so I did. I believe the box is at least thirty-five years old; it might be closer to forty. It's in pretty good shape for a much-travelled, middle-aged cardboard.

The Bass box within the Nike box holds a blue plastic container with "Johnson Baby Wash Cloths" across the top. It's possible my mother used them, but I know I did after my son was born. They were a staple for a short time in the car and the diaper bag. The container likely dates from 1990 or 1991. My mother died in 1988.

There are samples of Maggie's Organic Cotton, a company launched in 1992—so they aren't right too—and a vertical roll of thread with needles, the kind of travel sewing kit my ex-husband would have picked up on a business trip. There are Singer Iron-on Patches—and spools of Woolworth's Size 50 Polyester thread. They could be my mother's. But I have also used iron-on patches on blue jeans of all shapes and sizes for years, long after she was dead. I am not sure about the Dritz Glovers/Leather Hand Needles for $1.39 or the Heavy Duty Snaps from EZ International for $4.00. Hers or mine?

I put the lid on the Nike box and take in what is now clear—and probably has been for years. The box isn't hers. Every time I've grabbed a needle and spool of dark thread to replace a button, mend a hem, stitch a rip in someone's slacks, it's possible I was using a remnant from her, but more likely, was using something that I (or someone else) acquired over the years. Does it matter that not all in the box is hers? Everyday activities, life changes, random shopping have likely added to or subtracted from it. A generation has passed and another is passing—moves across country and from one home to another have occurred since she could have used the box. Maybe it started out as her box but now is something else. For me, if something in the box is hers, it is still something of her I have. But what if none of it—what if nothing in the box is or ever was hers?

Sewing is something she did, and by holding onto her sewing paraphernalia or some vestiges of it, I have kept part of her with me. Inside the box, I see the accoutrements of her sewing self.

Underneath the window behind the dining table was a dark-wood console that held the Singer sewing machine. It sat next to the traditional wood hutch with the china and silverware, platters and glasses, used for guests and holidays. The drawer on the left side of the console held a tape measure, marking chalk, bobbins for the machine. At the end of a sewing session, she could fold the machine into the table—and the top would become a repository for stuff, fabric or patterns or the detritus of everyday life, until the next time she needed to sew. She lined drapes or made curtains, replaced a hem, sewed a shirtwaist dress, and sometimes she'd show herself through an unexpected spark of color or an embellishment. She never taught me to sew—I'm not sure why—maybe she figured I wasn't the sewing type. Or maybe I was and it was just one more thing we missed in each other. Maybe I keep the needles and thread that I believe belonged to her to connect to what might have been.

There was also a small red wicker sewing box, and I have no idea what happened to it. I only remember the Nike box (or thought I did), so I claim it. It's what I have.

2020

In Spring, in pandemic lockdown, I take on a massive clean-up. In a back bedroom, I lift the top of a very old cupboard, which I might not have opened in twenty years, and there is the pin cushion in the shape of a large strawberry, a small berry dangling from the top to make sure we get what we are seeing, straight pins with tiny silver, blue, and black tops stuck in it.

It's inside my mother's sewing box, a beige box with a lid that does not have any company branding on it. I have no idea what the box originally held, but it is stuffed now. In it, among other things, are Clarke's Hand Sewing Assortment (needles) for 80 cents; two maroon Nouveaute buttons for 27 cents; an unopened packet of White Bias Tape (5 yds) for 25 cents; a bright green zipper; a small white envelope of extra shirt buttons; black cutting shears, so worn the black enamel is stripped away, revealing silver underneath; a paper bag from Monique Fabrics with buttons from La Mode for 60 cents; Yards of Name Tape with my sister's name on it, addressed to Robert Shearer (my father), not to my mother, a choice she often made; White 1/2 inch elastic straps from Sears; a No 675 Dritz Dressmaker's Marking Pencil; the stub of a 555 Anchor Superite No. 2 pencil; a receipt from Fabric Circle from 10-11-76 for two buttons ($1.26 with tax); a square of woven/textured purple fabric, a range of distinctive stitch types sewn across it. I have a vague remembrance of it—but can't remember what the fabric was used for. My mother sewed a purple dress with a short lavender jacket for me when I was about 12 or 13—is it that? The color feels right; the fabric doesn't, too heavy for a springtime dress.

There are also spools and spools of Talon thread in bright pink, lavender, coral, light blue, gold as well as all the expected blacks, browns, whites, and grays, and an empty spool for color 905 (which Google tells me is orchid).

I'm curious about the box, but I don't know if I can embrace it as my mother's. The other box—the Nike box in its longtime place on the shelf in my closet—is already my mother's sewing box. That it is really an emblem, not an artifact of my mother's life, has little sway.

I take out items one by one, carefully look through them, and then put them back in the box. I can't fit the lid over the top. The strawberry pin cushion sits up too high, letting me know the items in the box can't be hidden away. If I open the cupboard, they'll be there. They'll be visible.

I don't know why I am unhappy to find this box. It could be a relief. Instead, it feels like one more thing to carry—to have to navigate truth when I was certain of reality. I'd prefer to stay with what I thought was real instead of what is. I put the box back inside the cupboard. I close the top. I know now my mother's sewing box lives, but I've already made a connection to, I am already attached to, the fictional, maybe I should say, fabricated one.

I tell myself it is a time when accuracy matters—when we need to rely on fact (not the big lie, fake news, partial truth)—and here I am shying away, resisting it.

And yet—~~does it really matter which one I hold on to?~~

There is also this—What if neither the Nike Box nor the Beige Box are really my mother's? What if the amalgam of things added to or taken from them over time make them something else or something new? I have this nagging feeling about the strawberry pin cushion—was it really hers? It feels right to say so, but I don't have a reliable memory of it and can't actually place it with her. What if it's mine—and years ago, for whatever reason, I placed it with her things and now I can't separate it from them?

I remember after her long illness the quickest of deaths—and a rapid giving away of things. When or how the box got from her closet to the cupboard or how the other shoebox became my substitute for it, I have no idea and have no desire to probe remembrances or uncoil memories. I'd like to have something to look at and think "a piece of my mother is imbued here"—and it's not that simple. Some facts are clear; some realities aren't. That's what's true.

A Definition for Creatives: The Chance to be Reflective While Making Work; Being Aware of What Lets Us Progress (or Not)

I created a work-in-progress series. I had this idea that writers learn to write, in part, by being able to name what their choices are and then make them. I wanted to show how I reflected on choices and made decisions as I was creating work. Years ago, I started writing a novel and keeping a journal (as a part of the artmaking process) detailing how I wrote the novel (showing what I considered and how I made choices in developing the work). No one encouraged me to do it. A psychologist friend told me not to do it—that I'd ruin the work by overanalyzing it. I'd imagined a fun interplay—it was the era of meta-fiction—between an insider perspective, warts and all, and the burgeoning story—a woman long an adult but still caught in family dynamics, "running" away from home and sending her mother (occasionally) and her brother (more often) postcards. She wanted to be in touch with them but also wanted to limit how much she disclosed to them—and it was the 1980s. Long-distance phone calls were expensive. I was thinking of postcards more than fifteen years before I ever made them. In this novel, the reader only saw the text and taglines that suggested image; it never occurred to me to make them.

I did work on the book, but I got lost in the idea of it more than the runaway's story. Eventually, I put it in a stationery box and filed it away. What has stayed with me is the question of what is known/knowable in the artmaking process.

In "The Showbox Sewing Box," I use image as a conduit to relational play—between what is unknown or can't be known in my life—and what can be shared, if not fully known, about writing. I include a line that I strikeout (~~does it really matter which one I hold on to?~~) because the question doesn't feel right to me. Of course, it matters. That's why I am writing about it; even if the question is less which to hold onto but what. I am trying to decide so many years after death—what remnants do you carry with you? What do you let sit in a box and never look at? What gets mixed up with other memories or with the rest of our life and so becomes its own thing or becomes something we don't recognize at all?

As a writer what is true for me is my responsibility to be as accurate as possible, to note what is real or imagined and call it what it is. Another is to name as much as possible what I see—through what I observe (via memory or sight)—and to realize the questions inherent in what my seeing shows me. Sometimes I explore them and sometimes I just let them live unbidden because to stay with the question or to sit with the uncertainty or ambiguity it raises is too much or too hard. The strike-out stays—and I re-frame it. I leave it open ended.

I am in a phase of life where there will be less collecting over time and more getting rid of, cleaning out, shredding what there is and limiting what I hold onto. Physically, I don't need all I have.

My mother did not have this stage of life. She was dead by the age I am now. She didn't get the chance to cull through her belongings, decide what to keep or what to discard. We didn't talk about who gets to go through your drawers? There was nothing startling or, by many people's criteria, very revelatory in them except it was all hers. I think she would have liked that her sisters and my sister got to go through her jewelry or take some shoes or a dress or skirt. She would have enjoyed they took romance novels or biographies or history books. She would have been fine with someone taking her recipes, though many were from others' cookbooks. In what is there is also what is not. She didn't often write down recipes for what she cooked; what she liked to make, she took with her to the grave. She didn't leave a file of doctor's notes or medical records either—all she knew she took with her.

The sewing boxes are a question—Where is she in them? Is she? Bits of her, yes, in the objects and in my memories. In that blur of or borderline between what was and what is remembered she is also there. How much or with what degree of accuracy? All I can own is the question and my desire for an answer. The ambiguity is tension.

I understand the tension cannot be resolved by rejecting or disregarding facts—my mother's sewing box or not-sewing box is my connection to that.

New ending—or if I were to write this again—the boxes and what is in them is present tense. I don't want to go too far back and probe what got deleted or forgotten or neglected or dumped into the box. Her death was an inciting event in a story of change/transition. I have lived too long in what I might have been or might have been able to give to her—and simply the boxes show that along the way I was okay with mixing things up, of bringing aspects of others in, and letting all kinds of things enmesh themselves with us—that it was not her or me, or her and not me, it was us.

Does it matter if I align with one shoebox over the other? Yes and no—but also not so much. Seeing through that lens is clarifying.

I have not answered my question, but I have tried to. I'm okay with that.

Resources

Definitions

Postcard: https://www.etymonline.com/search?q=post
Sustainable: https://dictionary.cambridge.org/us/dictionary/english/sustainable#
Remnant: https://www.dictionary.com/browse/remnant

Book and Article

Allen, Pat B. (1995), *Art is a Way of Knowing*, Shambala.
I explore art as poetic offering in Hof, Kerstin (editor), (2020), "Offerings: a Poetic Approach to Text and Image." *Dreierlei Mut. Collagen zur Relevanz von Poesie, Literatur & Schreiben in Gesellschaft & Gesundheit,* Berlin: Germany: HBP University Press.

Reflection and Exercises

This chapter offers tools on mending, relationship, and offering. I hope you'll reflect on them as you write, using, adapting or altering them for your work. Here, I want to offer two exercises—Go Shopping and Start Again —and the chance for you to make a postcard. They focus on ways to help you reaffirm and sustain your practice as a writer. The final section of the Start Again exercise invites you to explore writing is relationship.

I also want to offer two understandings that you might want to use as tools:

- Writers write. What do you see when I say that? When do you know you are writing? What does being a writer who writes mean to you?

- You get to choose what you say. What are you ready (as a person and craftsperson) to say— go with that. Reach, dream, believe but also see where you are as writer. Inquiry, curiosity, understanding yourself are important to that. Who you are right now—please let that be in dialogue with what you want to create.

Go Shopping Exercise

Think of yourself as an artist's studio. Fill yourself with all the materials you need. Touch and hold them. Experiment and play with them. What results? When writing is art, how does what you construct renew you? How does it shift your perspective, alter your experience, allow you to emerge anew?

Ten Not-So-Tangible Tools for Writers, mixed media, 2001

One of the things I enjoyed most about making work of text/image was going shopping, stepping into an art store, walking the isles, and taking it all in. As someone who had never worked in the visual arts before I started making postcards, I was learning along the way. I touched pencils, papers, oil pastels, tacky glue, acrylics, gloss and matte mediums, canvas and hardboards, wood and Papier-Mâché boxes, X-Acto knifes, cutting mats, and much, much more. I used what I used—and kept adding to what I had, so the work could continue to develop and grow.

Imagine your writing/art space. See what is already there. Envision what you'd like to have. Then please go shopping. Find an art store, a store that sells art supplies, a bookstore that sells the journals or notebooks or writing supplies you love. Take a walk through the aisles. Buy something that you'd like to use right now --or (right now) don't buy anything at all. Just walk the aisles--pay attention to what intimidates you and what appeals.

Then, walk through your home, your yard, a park, a grocery or home-goods store, a bead or fabric store, and look for materials you'd be willing to work with. Look for pencils, pens, pieces of cardboard, fresh flowers, buttons, thread, jewelry (you can take it apart or cut it up), string or leather scraps, fabric from old clothing, used books or magazine covers, articles you might cut up, photographs, stones. Collect what you might be willing to use or draw from.

Set out your purchase and your found items. Notice all the materials you can bring to your work. Collect what you might be willing to use or draw from. If you want to try text/image work or to play with ways that visual materials can benefit your writing, great. But this is your imagining, and you can do with it what you want. You can let the colors and textures and every day or exotic objects speak or inspire or influence you, and you don't have to work with them directly at all. Let them remind you that our work begins in what and how we see, but we can construct our seeing however we want.

A through line of this book is that our images give us access to our stories, to the ones we want to tell, to the ones we don't or can't, but also access to how they influence us. They tell us what we want to reach for or imagine—we can use them literally in the work—and/or we can use them to support us in our writing.

After you complete this exercise, describe and/or draw your studio/workspace; include what it looks like and what it holds, the materials you have. Review what you've created, what do you see? What will you take from this exercise into your studio/workspace?

Note: You can do this exercise by shopping online, if you prefer, and simply looking around the room or space you are currently in. You can also imagine what you'd like to have if you prefer not to buy anything. Do this exercise in a way that feels right to you—that will best benefit you and your work.

Start Again Exercise (30–40 minutes)

Materials: blank paper or journal, pen or pencil. Optional: drawing pencil or colored pencils.

You can write or write/draw in this exercise.

Part One: An Important Writing Moment (8–10 minutes)

When did you first begin writing? Why? Remember the moment. Step into that time. Step into the person you were. Visualize it as a dynamic moment—and write/draw it as you are seeing it. Then review what you create. What stands out for you about how you felt? What did writing offer you? What was it for you? Make a list of some of the words that come to you.

Part Two: Quit Writing Moment (8–10 minutes)

Reflect on a moment when you wanted to quit writing or stop writing. Remember a moment when you did not want to write (or could not), a moment when you felt lazy or distracted or distant from your writing, a moment when you did not want to do the work, or your body/mind refused to write. Visualize the moment. Step into that time. Step into the person you were. Write/draw the moment. What made you stop your work? See that. Review what you've created. What words come to mind?

Part Three: Relate the Moments (8–10 minutes)

Please look at these two moments in relationship to each other. What is the same? What is different? What was missing for you in the Quit Writing moment that was in your Important Writing moment? How was your relationship to writing in each moment? What is one thing that distinguishes them?

Stay with both moments—and imagine yourself enjoying/engaging writing again. Try to reconnect with the person in the Quit moment. Imagine a way out of or beyond it for that person. If you can't see it clearly, what do you hope for? What could you do? How might you reconnect with the relationship you had with writing in the Important moment? Write/draw in response to any of the questions here.

If other writing moments come up as you write your Important Moment or your Quit Moment, feel free to note them, but don't dwell on them. Stay with the moments you've already focused on and see what they offer you.

Part Four Review and Reflect (10 minutes)

Please review what you've created above. What can you—or would you like to—rely on again when you want/need to reconnect with your relationship with writing? What if you let yourself quit—so you could start again? How might you do that? When I quit writing, drawing became a catalyst for how I could find my way back to writing, to sustainable practice.

What is your experience of meaning (or meaning making) in either or both moments? If so, please name, describe, or draw it. Consider how you can carry it forward, keep it as part of your work now.

What is an action or activity you might use to start again? Please list some (you don't have to be good at them to list them).

Reflection (5 minutes)

Review what you've created. What is (or might be) a starting over process for you? Also, what do you learn about what sustainability or meaning making might be for you? What image does sustainability evoke for you? Meaning making? Write or write/draw them.

I've learned I experience sustainability when (1) I take care of my relationship to writing and see myself for who I am at the time and in the moment when I am writing, and (2) I keep returning to what has meaning for me. When or how do you experience sustainability?

Next Step (Seven days)

Does what you've created here suggest new work? Is there something you want to make? Perhaps pick an important or quit moment, an important or quit image, your starting over process, an insight about sustainability— and write a draft. Reflect on your understanding of mending, relationship, and offering in your mind as you write. Let those tools inform your writing process. Review the draft then sit with it.

If you are willing to stay with this piece and keep working on it, try these things and then create another draft:

- In a week, return to the draft above and notice if the tools offered to you inform the writing. If so, how? What tools does the draft suggest are important to you? Name them and hold them in mind when you create a new draft.

- As you read, visualize an image of the relationship you want to have to with your writing in this draft. Draw that image or write a few sentences to depict it. Read the draft again. This time, visualize an image of your relationship to your reader. Draw that image or write a few sentences to depict it. What's the relationship between those images? List the qualities. Hold those qualities in your mind and draft your piece one more time.

- Read the new draft. How do you experience relationship as you read? How do the tools that you draw on inform the relationship?

Writing is Art Postcard Exercise (30–45 minutes)

For the exercise, you'll need a blank card. You can use a piece of cardboard or even plain paper cut to the size of a postcard. I like to use mixed media cards (6" x 8"), but any cardstock or paper with heft can work. Pencils, colored pencils, pens, markers, scissors, items for collage—all can be used. Decide for yourself how much you want to invest in materials. It's what you bring to the process that matters most.

Reflect on writing as art as a vacation from your usual writing/artmaking process. Why is vacation important to you? What image of vacation emerges? Where are you? What surrounds you? What do you see, smell, hear, touch? Place yourself in the vacation. Be there.

What from this vacation place do you want to share? What do you want to hold onto after you return home, especially when the writing gets hard or you don't think you can sustain it? What's your message? On one side of the card, please create an image or text/image and on the other share your message. Who are you writing to? Is the card for you to keep and refer to when you write? Or are you letting someone (one person or an audience) know how you see yourself as writer? Write your message and, on that side of the card, please make a stamp. Keep the card or share it, reflecting on which action will best support you.

3 STAY WITH IT

Memory Boxes in Words

Box 1: Staying With It. Possibility

Box 2: Practice

Box 3: Play and Curiosity

Box 4: Place/Peace

Box 5: Perspective/Vantage Point

After I created text/visual stories in boxes, I wanted to see if I could box experience relying only on words. I wanted to simplify memory, pare it down to what there was room for, while also filling the box with all that needed to be said. I was curious what a box could contain, what there wasn't room for. The five boxes presented here are a nod to and outgrowth of that project. Here I am playing with the idea that creative work, our art, is a container—we make it within the possibilities and limits of the container we choose. For me, considering the container (in these writings, box as a containing image) is as central to the artmaking as what I reach to see and depict.

When I first started introducing students to visual objects and words as materials for creating text/image work, I ordered sets of papier-mâché boxes. Like Russian nesting dolls, the boxes came in sizes, small and medium fitting inside the largest box. Each had a lid and space inside. They could take paint or collage or all kinds of glue and gel—and each student got to choose the size of their box, so they also had choice on the size of their story or the range of what they could share. For me, these choices are important even when the box is image, not object—how much can it take in and show? How does the possibility of the box—and its limits—shape what can be shared?

I like a box with lid, that can be opened or removed. When I think of a box I think of the contents as well as the structure that holds them, but I am also playing with "outside the box" while being very within the box. Box is also an adjective and a verb and has urban and slang meanings, but I've focused on it as a visual object and what each box can hold and what it cannot.

Box 1: Staying With It. Possibility

The Art of Fervor

"How can I contribute more?" I noticed right away Alonzo King, Artistic Director of LINES Ballet, didn't ask the dancers "How can you contribute more?" The difference between the two questions was subtle but sharp—Alonzo's approach is to ask the dancers to ask themselves.

I was lucky to be at Thursday rehearsal in Studio Five in the LINES Dance Center just two weeks before the San Francisco opening of Scheherazade. From my folding chair, I leaned into the space across the room from where the dancers stood in a circle around Alonzo. Then, in a voice less like directive and more like invitation, Alonzo asked them to give more to each moment—by not being tired or hungry, distracted, or overwhelmed—but by bringing more to the characters at the core of their movements. All looked right at him as he spoke.

It didn't surprise me that Alonzo focused on the inner performance rather than the physical one. In my conversations with him, he avoided labels offered to him such as choreographer or director. Instead, he identified as an artist—sure that all artists tap into and draw from the same creative sources whatever their mediums. Artists always have the chance to bring themselves all the way into their work, he believes, to not hold back, not resist, in every moment, to make a maximum contribution.

"If your character is not your temperament," he told one dancer, "then you'll have to overdo the moments." I understood him to mean this dancer will have to overreach to find the right tone or expression for his movements. If he doesn't overreach, he won't be able to get far enough outside himself to find the genuineness of the character within.

The lesson applies widely to artmaking. To make art beyond ourselves, we need to reach within and be willing to extend beyond ourselves. Deep within to find the clarity necessary to communicate a moment or feeling, an action or process. Beyond ourselves to feel and experience the contrasts necessary to locate a character within us or the character of what we want to convey.

Alonzo's approach speaks to the value for artists, as learners and professionals, in training and practice, to speak across the disciplines to each other. "I want to see change," Alonzo said. Looking at two of his dancers, he said, "I need to see the character within your movements." He talked about how, for a character to work, both clarity and contrast must be visible. He might have been teaching a fiction writing class.

"We need fervor." The dancers looked again intently into his face. "Does that make sense?" He asked this several times during the afternoon—did they get the meaning? He knew they needed to understand the meaning of what he was asking, of the opportunity offered them through dance, to achieve it.

After rehearsal, I looked up *fervor*. Not surprisingly it means two somewhat-related things: (1) warmth or glow—a radiating heat, and (2) intense heat—intensity and heat. Its meanings come from the Latin *fervor* meaning "heat" and *fervere* to "glow, boil." Fervor heats from within and moves out.

Fervor is the artist's path to clarity and contrast. Clarity radiates out, obliterating line or space between the person and the character, the story and the performance, the dancer and the dance. Contrast is conflict. An intense heat within stories, characters, and our layers of being that unsettle us and require us to act. Fervor manifests art, taking us beyond the process of contribution to the act of commitment. With fervor, we contribute all we can.

Alonzo asked the dancers to give more and when they did, he acknowledged what he saw. "There—that intensity," or "you had it when you started," he said. As the dancers moved across the floor, I could hear him say, "Stay with it. Stay with it. Don't relax."

"It brings me joy to see people change. It gives me hope for myself," he said as he returned to his chair. Five, six, seven, the music started again and so did the dance. "Stay with it. Stay with it," I thought to myself. "Don't relax."

I like being in rehearsal; a place similar but also different from where I and the range of artists I know practice. It provides a place to work out what is being made, where, as artists, we can test out what it will take to make what we want and decide if or how we can get there. A place for possibility. Inside rehearsal at LINES, I value the opportunity to witness what others do, to take it all in. I also like to learn from difference, to take in something new. For me, curiosity leads to learning; together they provide the origins for possibility.

I see how the dancers keep their legs warm or how they interact before the moment or music starts, how as they wait, they care for their body or mind or heart or find a corner to run through their movements or a sequence of steps. Many things have stayed with me all these years—that the practice space has a tone (attentive), that skill is visible but so is commitment; commitment invites a relationship between dance and dancers and allows for openings or options in the work.

Possibility, I've learned, is not a given; it needs designated space, requires attention to relationship. Years ago, I was given a scholarship to a workshop. I sat with writers, directors, producers in a room, dim like the LINES studio. The workshop leader, known for an award-winning script, shouted, haranguing a middle-aged woman, an accomplished writer, whose script we were reviewing. She stayed through his tirade, and we all waited for it to end, but she rightly told him what she thought of how he spoke to her. The rest of us said nothing. Later in the week, I met with the writer to discuss my script, and he was kind. He liked my sassy teenage character, her grandmother, and the road trip that changed their relationship, but I couldn't take in his comments. I respected his accomplishments but not his actions and was disappointed with myself for not being able to say that. With two days left, I ended up writing mostly on my own. The tensions I couldn't resolve distancing me from other mentors and writers in the community.

Not all is exactly right in the LINES Studio; some things are still being worked out. The work is progressing, even if slightly more slowly than wanted—or maybe needed. Soon the company will move to the theater for final rehearsals, but no one is on the verge of being silenced or harmed. Everyone can speak. Respect, evident in the space, feels essential for possibility.

My colleague Kris Brandenburger says conversation across the arts in the presence of art opens art and artists to possibility. My use of that word comes from her. The conversation, which I think of as dialogic inquiry, lets artists connect and imagine. I care about what another's work provokes inside me. For me, there isn't a direct or one-to-one correlation between my work and another's in a different art medium or form. What works, what is exciting, what I think is true is that conversation incites something that we can choose to probe more. Alonzo shares what he means by maximum contribution and fervor, but ultimately what I think matters is what does his way of talking, moving, shaping work, engaging the dancers evoke or provoke in me when he speaks about them? Can I stay with it? Have I? I am still asking those questions. The inquiry incited by my work with Alonzo is active; it also inciting this book.

Earlier in 2010, we met in the Odd Fellows building (7th and Market), where LINES rents space and studios. The building has housed the Independent Order of Odd Fellows since 1909; I hear the building is now for sale, like so much in San Francisco is since the pandemic. The interior was dark; it had no pretense. There is a person-operated elevator and large and small studio spaces on several floors. The MFA students, a few faculty, and I entered a large studio, not the space where the company rehearses, a space for dance classes and smaller rehearsals. Alonzo led a workshop for all of us. We were writers, dancers, performers, a musician, a photographer, painters, mixed-media artists, poets.

He had the expectation that all of us would dance—and we did. What would happen when we all moved, if everyone had the experience of dance and then we reflected on it? That was the core question of the workshop. One definition of dance involves moving the body and feet to music, another to move the body quickly and lightly. For me it was to move as practice in possibility, to move with intention, to show what movement could be and what it might show us about ourselves.

We didn't learn Western Classical Dance. We learned to move with and push through the imaginary. We waited on one side of the studio, and when prompted, would hop or glide, reach or sway, rush or even run to the other side. We were aware of our feet, legs, hands, faces. Alonzo noticed if we gave ourselves to the movements. In that way, he was no different with us than he was with his LINES dancers. We learned to sequence our movements. We became aware of rhythm and an eight-count, asking ourselves what we could contribute, in space and across time, to the evolving story within the dance.

Alonzo showed us, movement-by-movement, how to construct a dance. One of the early gestures involved putting our fists through a solid wall. Alonzo, his body still but energized, imagined the wall—and its messy, muddy texture. He took his right hand and quietly turned and turned it until I felt like I could see wet, pasty dirt dripping off his arm and his hand boring steadily through the wall. Alonzo's deep imagining transcended his body and made the wall—and the gesture—feel real. Nothing changed for him. His body was all in, but what I saw invited me to imagine what I was seeing, a hint of what could be seen was all that I needed to be able to imagine it. Like Eliott, I was overhearing the experience and, therefore, could imagine beyond it.

And—Alonzo was showing us—skill is not just training, it is capacity. In his essay "Art Thought," he says we often understand it as a "display of powers," (2011, 87), but actually we "want to do what's required to create what is needed. What you are interested in is making ideas clear . . . It is the mental ability and the heart's capacity that has to be huge. It is the mind and heart that dances, sings, and plays—not the body" (King 2011, 87). I simply let the experience speak to me. I see how moments of movement and stillness work together, and I wonder how I make that dance on the page.

Alonso refers to art as intelligence, a "knowing" beyond "inference and deductive reasoning" within all of us that "has no limits to its diversity of expression" (2011, 86). Working with Alonzo helps me to understand forms of art are inherently connected to each other through the range of and difference in what we make and why. The shared knowing we experience as artmakers (and humans) places us in relationship with others; we're community linked by the capacities that artmaking gives us and ways to express it, not just makers in our disciplines. When we talk with each other, we can see beyond the forms we work in and into the knowing that art arises from them; we see those we are in conversation with and ourselves more fully.

As viewers, we also decide what we see. For me, dance as an experience takes me so far outside myself that it allows (or forces?) me to see literally from a different space and perspective. I can hold it with fear or with possibility. It connects me to sense and memory—and though I view what is happening on the stage, I connect with what resonates for me— and that becomes my experience of the dance. In 1979, I had a class with Paul Thompson, at the time a resident director of the National Theatre in London, author of *The Children's Crusade* and *The Lorenzaccio Story*, who taught at Antioch. Paul drew on the Stanislavsky Method for how he worked. There is one line in a series of poems I wrote, based on one of Paul's exercises, that stands out for me:

trust
    gesture only

It spoke to the physicality required in performance and dance—but also how movement via hand or feet or face or other parts of the body can convey who someone is and what the moment offers. I realized, as a writer, I needed to see every gesture a character made. I needed to link gesture and action, gesture and intention, gesture and the moment when writing a scene. Visualizing was key to that. It was a first understanding for me of what I could absorb from another art and bring to my work.

Again, I am not saying as I learn to experience or engage with an artist who moves or uses a camera or paints or draws or makes collage that I will necessarily take the specifics of the process (or the materials) into my work. The power and the benefit, I believe, is that I can hold artmaking from a multi-perspective/multi-materials way—that the shifts are subtle—it is more like osmosis, as the *Cambridge Dictionary* says, "the ways in which ideas and information gradually spread between people." I absorb it and it somehow adds to or shifts something in me.

I talk with a sound artist about the difference between sound and sonic—and I am now curious about the idea of sound as movement and vibration (and maybe how it influenced what Elliott's overhearing was). What will I do with it? I don't know, but the exposure changes me. It provokes new questions or asks me to see questions I already have differently. It adds to my artmaking; it influences me and has impact. In my work, I'm so focused on the visual—on what we can see—but this conversation opens a new possibility—What do I need to hear to make my work? How does my experience of sound influence how I want or need to bring sound to the page? Maybe my next inquiry will be away from the visual and into how hearing shapes our work.

I've learned to let all artists be teachers to me. Some, like Alonzo, I gravitate to personally, philosophically, aesthetically. My exposure to others offers me insight about medium or form. For example, in a workshop for our MFA students, I listened to Gene Luen Yang, author of *American Born Chinese*, talk about constructing text/image panels in the graphic novel. One thing I heard him say is text and image can always work in one of two ways—(1) text can convey emotion or feeling and image can convey story or (2) image can convey emotion/feeling and text can convey story (keep the story moving). Do I use a text bubble, "In fifteen minutes?" and provide an image of a kitchen with a burnt chicken on the counter, smoke still swirling, and a mess of half-chopped potatoes and vegetables strewn over the counter and the floor, no person visible. Or do I show an image of a frazzled character in a stained apron hanging up the phone and a scream in the dialogue box? The insight is a tool—and I ask myself does it hold up? Did I understand what I heard him saying? Is that always the way it is—and so I look for that when I am reading or viewing? But more important to me—I carry the importance of the relationship—between what can be seen (and what can be said) into my work. It helps me to think visually, the way considering gesture as I describe above does. Both spark inquiry—if I only have words to use, how do I get this visual effect with language?

In *Drawing the Surface of Dance: A Biography in Charts*, choreographer Annie-B Parson tells us she makes charts to document dance after it has been performed. She lets other art forms influence her (writing, visual image and materials, design). For me, her charts illustrate possibility. They include a short statement (or summary) and a visual representation, a drawing or drawing/collage or photos and/or a sequence of all those things. The charts are a "a graphic digression . . ." and vary for each work: "The shape of the chart is a new choreographic structure. The charts are their own dance piece where the proscenium stage is the horizon line of your eyes, and the floor is made of paper" (Parsons 2019, 8). The chart is a record for her—and engagement for us—and for me a catalyst to think about the inter-arts ways that as writers we can document our work. I ask myself, if I were to draw or collage a record of my work, what would I include and why—and how might it become its own piece?

Again, for me, exposure creates possibility. Another example: Alonzo and I designed another workshop for MFA students in my Interdisciplinary Arts Workshop. In the class, I was using a newly published book of letters/postcards between Gertrude Stein and Picasso, Lynn Nottage's play *Intimate Apparel*, letters play a key role in the play, excerpts from *Frida Kahlo's Diary* (in particular, Plate 11, a letter to herself), Gary Snyder's sweet poem, "A Letter to M.A. Who Lives Far Away," and some other pieces. I also asked students to collect letters meaningful to them, any kind of letter, personal, business, notecards, unsent letters, and to look up the meaning of the word *letter*. I had this idea that students would make letters in some way and collaborate on how to present them, using movement, a very text-driven way of thinking about it.

I was focused on the physical objects, but Alonzo saw the body. He wondered—what if we asked them to think about letters, like letters in an alphabet (A, B, S, C, for example) and they could draw from the letters within the letters (or the words within the letters). What if they danced letters, using their bodies to shape the alphabet that forms the written words? Such play, such fun.

He said we could consider the rhythm and tone/mood of correspondence. What if they thought of the letters as musical score? He asked—what is the rhythm within a letter when read aloud? Or when read in silence? How does the rhythm or music or sound of a letter change as the reader comprehends it? What is the sound or rhythm of difficult sentences in relationship to ones that flow or are easy to take it?

He began to imagine and then describe how the body could make letters and how collectively the group could work together to form letters as message or code or as part of a phrase or sentence—and to connect to the meaning and experience of letters themselves. His framing, his curiosity, his questions made what was possible—wonderfully so—different than what I imagined.

There are other acts of practice that can lead us to possibility for use of language in our work. For example, during pandemic lockdown, Christian Marclay took photos of empty, shuttered spaces in London and his friend Steven Beresford composed music in response to them. In their book, *Call and Response*, the music leads, the notes, like Alonzo's letters, have rhythm and tone and direct how we see the relationship between the composition and the photograph and, ultimately, how we read the photograph. When I look at the book, I can imagine how the notes sound, what the rhythm and feel of the piece is—and that imagining influences/shapes my experience of the photographs. As practice, what if we thought of our writing as musical composition—as a set of notes with properties beyond words?

As a writer, in part because of my work with Elliott Coleman, I have noticed every word and asked about and engaged in reflection on its need or benefit on the page. Now I am also aware of every letter and what it might be. That letters have movement and shape and sound inherent in them—and that might add to their performative capacity. Possibility—and awareness—an expansion of what might be. That is what the inter-arts offers me.

Box 2: Practice

Taking Doing into Being (2011)

At first, inside Kerner Studios in San Rafael the minutiae were all about lighting. I was getting a behind-the-scenes look at the filming of Alonzo's *Triangle of Squinches,* by 3SAT, a German Public Broadcasting

Company who was planning to televise it across Europe. A young woman in blue jeans and green T-shirt stood perfectly still in front of the set. The set is a long line of shimmering cords on moveable stands. Then she took a step over, waited again, got a command, and took a step back. She moved up and across the stage until every position for lighting was checked. Crew members also fetched a tall ladder and adjusted or changed lights around her. Smoke clouded everything—and when big black fans didn't blow it through fast enough, a man in cargo shorts took a large board and fanned the space. There were whispers and comments about a costume check—and "she is sewing it" right now. Alonzo sat before a bank of monitors, a microphone in hand—twice he used it to get Arturo and Laurel's attention. Cameramen adjusted their angles—while a large woman in a sleeveless T-shirt swept and mopped the Marley floor. Dancers stood at the side of the stage—they wore sweatpants and warm-up jackets—one dancer kept a thick scarf around his neck. The floor clean and tested dry, they picked spots on the stage. They practiced specific movements. A soundtrack alive in their heads, they focused on being performers, precise, unaware of the other dancers, the film crew, or a looming audience. The director called out, "I need for you to pull out of there." No one moved—and I had no idea who he was talking to.

I enjoy observing details, preparations, techniques—seduced by them into the space. They are often what we think art is. As artists, we want information, habits, and techniques and to be able to use them well. We need to practice the steps, know how to adjust the camera, set and re-set the lights. Using words well, solid brushstrokes, strong lines, the correct embouchure—we want to do these things right. We tell ourselves they are the essence of artmaking. Yet once a clapboard marks the scene and the dance begins—art is more than doing. It is taking doing into being.

I am using *being* in the sense of fullness of self—a quality of existence, not just being as existence. In artmaking I need to be aware of my existence, so I am present to and a presence in the making. When my existence is in relationship with my process and actions, I can be with what is made. Doing feels more like task to me—I do the dishes—while being suggests encompassing, a richer experience—I am being with my family right now, I am being with my work right now, I am simply being. In dance, Alonzo wants dancers to move beyond task to fullness, asking themselves—am I all the way in the work right now? That all-in-ness is being.

That day—more than ever—perhaps because I was a spectator, able to sit so close to the dancers and watch them move from preparation to performance, I saw how Alonzo does this: By requiring dancers to be, he makes ideas move. That's why I believe he refers to his dances as thought constructions. He is making thought move. Every movement on the stage is an idea or a metaphor in motion. Art is not a technical rendering but an embodying of being via doing. Doing, as an inquiry (as a curiosity), rather than simply as action, leads to being.

Take one: A dancer entered—she plucked the strings and then spreads them apart, stepping through the opening to the other side. Another dancer silently moved in. He stopped, stood tall, still, and watched—fully taking in her experience—watching and listening were silent movements within him. Then he moved toward her and together they pulled one panel of the radiant string apart from the others.

Alonzo constructed the dance so it replicates our ongoing choices as people (and writer/artists)—a dancer walked toward the string—engage it or not? Pull or strum it? Separate it and step through or step back? I noticed how often in the dance one dancer moved and another watched—moving us, as viewers, to think physically and emotionally—we are always alone and always with each other. What springs us to action? Often in this dance—sound—children laughing, revving motors—ignite movement. I noted two other things: (1) mirroring—one dancer moves and then another repeats the movement by making it his or her own; and (2) call and response—one dancer moves and the responder's movement reflects his or her listening to that. I learned Alonzo does not create male and female roles. He creates ideas that manifest in movements, and any dancer can do them. In writing, we use language as body—how it sees, touches, hears, tastes, to make ideas move.

In this dance, the movements build and repeat—so do the thoughts. The more we see the movements, the more the ideas reveal themselves to us. Alonzo constructed the work in this way—as if saying, don't worry if you don't get the message the first time, you'll have more chances. The dancers are moving our hearts and minds as well as our bodies. As they move through takes two, three and four, we are moved too. We break for lunch, knowing that if we have allowed the work to be in us, we are movers, thought constructors too.

Articulation, Not Such a Beautiful Word

In *Reclaiming Artistic Research*, Expanded 2nd Edition, artist Ryan Gander says traditional views on practice as repetition are "shuttering" and go against what art is: "The idea is to get better. It's a trajectory that moves over two and three decades. I think that's what you can call practice. . ." (Cotter 2024, 386).

I think inherent in what Gander is saying is to use practice to get better we need to try to articulate it, to say what it is, what frames it and the values that guide it. Alonzo identifying his work as thought constructions; his insistence on maximum contribution and being, not just performing the work, are ways of articulating it. Articulation provides a reference point for developing, altering, adding to, or revising our practice. We can't change what we aren't aware of; we limit our development unless we can recount (drastically or otherwise) what we make and why. Like practice, what we know likely moves over the lifespan of our artmaking, so articulating is a process that also moves as our work moves over time. For example, when I first started to draw chairs, I noticed I always drew two—and I got it early on. I was interested in putting two things in relationship in my work, but the more I drew and then the more I began to construct objects as well as draw, I noticed the objects were different, in contrast, opposite to each other. Inherent in what I made was often, if not always, a duality. Once I recognized this, I could play with it, and I did. Noticing it and being curious about it let me take new directions in my work. I got interested in disparate things— things that did not seem to go together but I felt did. "Yellow Room" is an example of the that. The yellow rooms, Soane's and mine, were easily relatable, but the psychic telling me that Elliott after his death was visiting me, I had to step more deeply into the experience and find its relationship.

Articulating is not a beautiful word, but I like it because within its meaning is the idea of clarity, trying to be clear—and it leaves open that we might try to be clear but may not succeed and that is okay. Articulating lets us see if we are practicing (present tense) or if our practice is just what has already been practiced. I've also experienced it as a valuable side benefit of conversation across the arts. If, as we share our work with artists working in other forms, we can also try to teach them about it, they can more fully join us in exploring and developing it. We also continue to teach ourselves, maybe adding to our clarity about what we are trying to make—and the possibilities for it. We create a shared understanding for others and us to work from.

Articulation does not tell us what we have to do; it offers us the chance to name and understand what we reach for in our work. When Alonzo, for example, articulates how he sees what might be possible in our workshop using letters, I get it and I get the chance to become more articulate about two things in my work—the limits of my knowing and the range of my work—and possibilities I was not aware of before and something new to explore. I get the chance to articulate what is and what might be.

A great teacher for me has been the poet, philosopher, and cultural theorist Judy Grahn. Judy and her partner, Kris Brandenburger, have been collaborators with me since we started the MFA program in 2009. Kris coined the term creative inquiry we use to ask students to probe the questions that are essential to their lives and artmaking—and Judy launched the first MFA in Creative Inquiry/Interdisciplinary Arts. When the university offering it closed, we reflected on their curriculum to create our MFA. In our program, we're curious about what writers/artists make and why. We're interested in what drives the writer/artist and the writer/art, the questions within the work. Through conversations with Kris and Judy, other faculty and, now, years of working with students, I've come to understand that, as makers, we can probe the questions inherent in our work in two ways—one, by trying to articulate them, and two, using what we learn from them to keep learning (viewing, reading, researching, talking with others, collaborating) so we keep getting to know them and can make decisions about how to work with them. I now think of inquiry as a curiosity-supported, process-driven play.

Grahn's "Introduction" to *love belongs to those who do the feeling* powerfully articulates her work. I love how willing she is to know herself as poet and citizen and thank her for how boldly she is willing to share what she knows with us. The essay names and situates her work, as writer and activist, in multiple contexts, including how, in 1969, she, Wendy Cadden, and five other women co-founded a "revolutionary movement—Gay Women's Liberation" and began publishing "women-centered and lesbian-formulated work" (2008, 15). She and Cadden also founded the Women's Press Collective in Oakland, California. The essay also locates her poetic intentions and practices—including how the poetry would "institute a ceremonial quality to being female" and, in "A Woman is Talking to Death" combines "personal and collective and historic experience, to reach out to make alliance with our communities" (2008, 17). She also tells us why "Mythic Realism" describes what she does in poetry: Shatter and transform Western myths so they become more real, more related to our lives, and appropriate to us (2008, 21).

The willingness to articulate who she is as writer and why allows her to describe "Some Ways of Knowing This Is a Judy Grahn Poem" (Grahn 2008, 18), a great gift but also a guide for reading her work. The list does not tell us what a Judy Grahn poem is but how we can recognize her poems. It helps us to join her in, maybe even search for, what she wants for the work, while we have our own experience of it. It is, however, not a static thing. This past winter I asked Judy to lead a workshop for our MFA students, and while she was with us, I asked her how she relies on that section of her essay now. She said she doesn't much—her understanding of the work, what she is trying to do, keeps evolving. The operative word may be "some." If her work is different now or has evolved beyond those 2008-identified ways of knowing, it still provides history or at least documentation we can rely on as we read. At lunch recently, we spoke about the vibrational quality of her poetry, articulating the sonic qualities within it and adding to my understandings of her uses of rhythm and sound, the musical aspects of her poetry. At 84, she continues to look within herself and to look at the world, working through a list of writing projects one by one. She is still interested in knowing her work and sharing that knowing. More than inspiring.

In the more than fourteen years since I first visited Alonzo's studio, the world and I have changed a lot—the financial impact on many universities has become much more intense and programs in the arts are much more disposable (Do we stay or do we go?). For me, as a writer/artist and educator, I feel the practice is to continue to try to understand the nature of what we do—and the range of what is possible—and make it visible for others.

Form as Practice

Form is a material that some writers/artists are using to make writing more visible. In some recent works of text and image, form is the practice. Richard Kraft in *It Is What It Is: All the Cards Issued to Donald Trump*, doles out five volumes of colored cards for Trump's infractions during his first term, just as a soccer referee would. Each card's color (red, yellow, orange, light blue, dark blue, among others) signifies Trump's unacceptable words or inappropriate actions, while Kraft's annotations and index detail them.

In *Ordinary Notes*, Christina Sharpe, offers 248 notes on the Black experience in America. Although the book's sections are each shaped by a different definition of note, the word *ordinary* complements the form via text, image, photographs, magazine covers, newspaper articles, excerpts from journals, letters, articles, and more. In section i, note is "a brief record of facts, though written down as an aid to memory" and in section viii, "to notice or observe with care" (2023, 1 and 349).

In *Diaries of War, Two Visual Accounts from Ukraine and Russia*, Nora Krug, a visual journalist, practices responsibility to truth and sensitively documents the perspectives of "my two protagonists, even when I didn't agree with them" (2023, 11). K and D, the two protagonists, recount their experience and Krug shapes it into a "consistent narrative" (2023, 6) that she illustrates after K and D approve her text. The form—visual and textual documentation, via illustration, design choices, and word—draws us into the contrasting narratives, leaving us to simply sit with what is said and shown. As we take it in, what will we do with it? That practice is up to us.

Box 3: Staying Curious—Play

2014

Alonzo invited me to LINES' creative residency and work-in-progress showing at Sonoma State University. In the new work. Alonzo was playing with the idea of a specter—an uncertain, unpredictable presence — hovering around the dancers.

On stage, he offered them this question: How can I be with whatever arises?

Early on, while my father could understand what I was asking him to sign, I got the documents needed—a will, a power of attorney, and two forms, a DNR and a POLST. After his years of Alzheimer's, him now in the end-stage of illness, I believed everyone understood no one was to resuscitate him. It was clearly written down and placed everywhere it needed to be. No one was to call a paramedic or an ambulance, no one was to take him to a hospital. He was not to be kept alive. As his caregiver, I'd done what was required to give him what he had always wanted in the last moments of his life—to die as simply as possible.

Instead, I was taking my morning walk, and a health-care aide at his memory care facility called to say my father was found not breathing, and they called the paramedics.

How *can I be* regardless of what arises?

I shouted into the phone, "No, no, no," running past the houses and dog walkers as fast as I could. "Do not resuscitate him," I yelled at her. I tried to move fast. I was at least twenty minutes from my home and car and then twenty minutes from him.

Then the aide broke in telling me the paramedics had tried to resuscitate him, but he had not responded. They would not do it again. They'd taken him to the hospital, now because he was dead.

The stage at Sonoma State was large, and I tried to see over the gray gap, maybe the orchestra pit, between my seat and where the dancers, technicians, and Alonzo rehearsed. I wanted to lean toward the question Alonzo was asking. The specter, muted like camouflage, was a shadow on the right side of the stage. I angled my body to the right as well to better focus on his movements, what happened in the space between him and the dancers.

Be here now.
Don't worry; be happy.
Let it be.

All those *be* and *being* phrases that infuse our culture filled my mind, and I looked away.

Be real, I wanted to say. Being with, being in, any kind of being felt like one more expectation, not something I could see or experience.

Alonzo's dance evolved, and it became quite different than what he and the dancers played with that first evening at the residency, but the image of the specter, a hazy figure on a dark stage moving stealthily, actions unclear and intentions invisible, stayed with me. Listening, Alonzo told the dancers, is an act of presence that transcends art forms. For days, probably for months, I couldn't really hear anything, let alone listen. All I could hear was a paddle against my father's chest—and that sound of trying to make him breathe. I did not want that. It took a long time before I could find a place for that image, and I could settle into the moments that happened next, the ones in which I live knowing that, even in death, I could not give him what he wanted.

Alonzo huddled with someone I couldn't see, the dancers took a break, and I thought about heading home. I was fidgety and tired. But I didn't really want to leave; Alonzo's invitation to be there, to be a witness to the work was genuine. Instead, I moved to the back of the theater. When they started again, I'd be able to see and hear from a distance.

How can I be regardless of what arises or whatever is around?

What I heard (finally) was how Alonzo brings together the word *arise* with the word *be*. To be, we let what arises move through us—from our artistic gut down to our feet or out to our hands or up our throats. Perhaps being is the ultimate grassroots arts activism, one that starts from our inner ground and finds its way through and beyond us to others. Alonzo told a dancer if he listened to his feet and weight that his movement would be more selfless and more real. Being takes us to the real.

"Play with it," Alonzo called out to a dancer moving among snowflakes that fall to the ground. Play feels like active listening, a way to sink into being. The aesthetic outgrowth of play is poetry, perhaps a poem in form but also poetry as a way of making. "Find the poetry," Alonzo said. One dancer intertwined herself with the legs of another until finally she rolled over his knees and onto the floor, freeing herself to be on her own so she could move away. One dancer pushed another on a rolling light fixture. He kept pushing while she negotiated the small surface she must stand on. Sometimes the dancers reached up as if they wanted to fly; other times they raised their arms in frenzy, their movements frantic and wild. The dancers showed me the search for being always exists within a sea of uncertainty and they are playing in movement to see what it might yield. Sometimes play is a serious thing, an act of improvisation and intention, tied to the most difficult things we navigate. Could I play with that moment between the beating and stopped heart? The dancers moved in pairs, with partners, or in the presence of another. Their connections were delicate but necessary. I was nowhere near the poetry of it all. Threat and uncertainty were hovering around.

But I did watch from the back row and look for the being in the dancers' movements. That didn't mean it was easy to take in. The specter existed. It was real. Dark things were present. Yet—in the edges of the moment, between then and what's next, so was the poetry the dancers manifested.

Alonzo didn't resolve the complexity for his dancers or me. His invitation was to play with and move through it. "You are already in it," he said to the dancers. "In it," he told them they had no choice but to move with all the layers of experience inside them, to let it arise and work through it as they danced. The same was true for me. Together, and on our own, would we move all the way through all that is?

I took a first step, moving again a few rows closer to the stage.

Writing is play.

Play with words, play with images, play with structures. Play with voices, perspectives, and strategies. Play right now if you want to. Go ahead. Just play.

Writing can be quite a task, a big commitment, more than you expected. It can be such hard work. It can also be vigorous and invigorating play. Follow what's hard or follow what's playful. All writing roads can take you to the location you want, to your place, or your destination.

Being playful is just more fun.

Ten-Not-So-Tangible Tools for Writers, text and mixed media, 2001

In London, in 1978–79, I'd take the Tube from Highbury/Islington to Tottenham Court Road and walk to the British Library. I went most days. I was on a quest to understand Gertrude Stein and the arts in Paris in the early 1900s. I sat in the Reading Room with my notebook and the day's requested books mostly exploring a question I heard Stein asking in *Tender Buttons*: Could she evoke visual objects simply through language? I also traveled to Paris to see the Museum of Modern Art and the Centre Pompidou, 27 rue de Fleurus, Shakespeare & Company and Montmartre. I wanted to be inside the art as much as possible to see if or how it might reveal something about how to make language visual.

Language as a still life, that's how I read *Tender Buttons*. If visual objects could be conveyed through language, what else could? I wondered if I could make a portrait—no visual image, only words. I tried; among them were "Portrait: Eleanor Marx," "Portrait: My Mother After the Kitchen Fire," "Portrait: The Man."

Making them was all play. I wanted to push the limits of words to find the limit (or the possibility) of what they could offer. I wanted words to be a vehicle of seeing—but also, I wanted to see if the cumulative effect of them on their own or in relationship to each other could show the reader what to see. In many ways the portraits failed; I'm okay with that word because although I learned that an intensive focus on using visual language has lots of positive benefits, including that visual language does make us see, I couldn't get the cumulative effect I wanted. I could evoke moments of seeing—and feeling about what the reader was being asked to see, but not a full portrait. Also, making the work was artistically fun. I used the page like a canvas or sketchbook. I used my typewriter (yes, portable typewriter in those days) like a pencil or paint. I focused only on

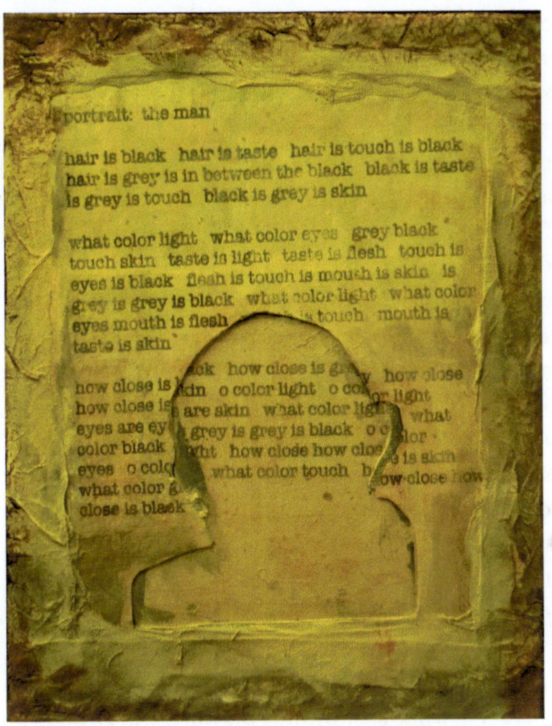

FIGURE 6 *Portrait: The Man*, Hardboard, 8" x 10", 2012.
Handmade paper, printed text, acrylic paint, oil pastels

the person I wanted to create and what I could see. My experience is acts of play don't always yield results right away, but they do yield them.

A side benefit: A re-offering project I took on was to re-make the portraits on hardboards. I started to include "Mother: After the Kitchen Fire," a very red piece with a female figure, a hole in her midriff and charred fabric all around. The dark edges make the play in it harder to see in a photograph. I choose "Portrait: The Man" for its imagist simplicity. It is a cut-out, a shadow, who the man might be lurks inside it. The cut-out rests on crumpled paper; in some places it is smoothed out, whatever that might mean. The focus is on the figure, the words shaping our impression of who he is. Which is the portrait: what we see or don't see? We can play with that.

Play for me is a way of engaging without intention; it's a loose-fitting rather than form-fitting way to work. I can play with words, materials, structures, ways of practice, any part of the artmaking process. It doesn't have to be experimenting; it is just a way of holding the grip more lightly, simply, a way of practicing with room to move. For writers, it might simply be trying to get the feel of the cut out, the crumpled paper, what can't be seen on the page with words.

Since I read *Tender Buttons*, I've been interested in how thinning the boundary between writing and visual art is valuable to writers. I've tracked the ways that writer/artists play with language and the relationship between text and image in graphic novels, visual essays, text/image work and in poetry, novels, memoir, artwork from small and independent presses as well as larger/commercial publishers. In recent years, I've gotten particularly interested in the works of writer/artists who work closely with designers or design-driven presses or write, make art, and design their books themselves, such as Jona Frank's *Cherry Hill*, Lauren Redniss's *Radioactive*, and Judith Schalansky's *Inventory of Losses*. I hope you'll explore their work.

Frank hired actors to play the people in her life, using writing and cinematic photography to re-tell/create her life including events that are imagined as well as what is lived/real. In *Radioactive: Marie and Pierre Curie, a Tale of Love and Fallout*, Lauren Redniss is at play in all aspects of bookmaking. She designed every aspect of the book, the cover and all pages in between, while also writing, drawing, and creating images for it. In *Inventory of Losses*, Judith Schalansky tells us the inter-play among writing, art, and design is what interests her: "The inseparability of form and content is the reason why I like not only to write, but also to design books" (2020, 24–5).

For me, these artists are asking us to consider how stories are offered to us—and what invites us into them. They are also inviting us to see the book as well as the writing and art within it. As technology makes us more visually aware and dependent, they are providing us ways to experience complex stories of loss, trauma, crisis, among many other things, through language, image, type, layout, color—adding to ways of connecting to readers.

The work is also serious play: My sense is the joining of writing, art, and design in bookmaking offers us new ways of engaging stories relationally, helping us to integrate the reality of our multi-layered lives, while also giving us moments of tangible relief (a handwritten note, a map, a mourning color, a dress that looks like wallpaper) from the intangibility (and the insecurity it evokes) within our everyday experience. Maybe it makes reading more pleasurable or comforting. I wonder, even if words are our sole medium, how we can aim for this.

In *Pocket Atlas of Remote Island: Fifty Islands I Have Not Visited and Never Will*, Judith Schalansky playfully tells us:

> It is high time for cartography to take its place among the arts, and for the atlas to be recognized as literature, for it is more than worthy of its original name: *theatrum orbis terrarum*, the theater of the world . . . Anyone who opens an atlas wants everything at once, without limits— the whole world . . . Give me an atlas over a guidebook any day. There is no more poetic book in the world (2010, 29).

What if, as writers, we begin to think of all writing as an inter-relationship among art, literature, and theater? How do we hold play and practice then?

I think she is reminding us that play is not just in the form of the work, but in the attitude it takes to make it. When I use the word *play*, I mean it in the sense of its origins in Old English *pleg(i)an*, exercise with freedom and intent. It lets the process within the practice go where it goes.

For me, play in writing/artmaking involves two things:

- *Let's see what happens*: An attitude toward making, a way of being in the work that suspends result or outcome.

- *Let's see what emerges*: A way of engaging or attending to art-making that lets the work find its way and me just follow its lead. Anne Bogart describes attending as what we give our attention to (Bogart 2007, 52–4).

Box 4: Place/Peace

At Home

Gale warning until Sun 9 PM. Rain 100% now through 10 PM

I hear it outside—rain, wind, a crash. Then my lights, clock, cable box, modem all shut down. I don't like the diminished access.

The wind pushes harder, and palm leaves bend, as if trying to touch the grass. Rainwater pouring from the roof is wet wind. It blows across the sliding door, flying away instead of splashing onto the ground.

My focus is on how I feel, as if what I want or don't want could have an impact on or might change the fact that at 9:49 AM my home feels like 5 PM. It's overcast inside and colder than it is outside.

I read Martin Gayford and David Hockney's *Spring Cannot be Cancelled: David Hockney in Normandy*. The work, so in contrast to my circumstances, captures me.

With so many glass doors and large windows, this house is a livable greenhouse when the sun is bright. Now it's more like being inside a light bulb turned off; a glass cloud cover darkens everything.

I check my phone, battery 53%. I've taken 869 steps, about 11,131 less than usual, to get water, clean the cat box, brush my teeth, wipe the kitchen counter, find a sweatshirt. With no power and the riotous rain, the farthest I might walk the rest of the day is outside, under the eaves of the roof, to the recycling bin.

I have a blanket and Alice, the cat, resting beside me. Every time I move, she jumps up and heads to her bowls to check for food or water then to the atrium door—to confirm the weather outside before she returns. I'd make tea, but I can't heat water. I want to eat but want more to keep what is in the refrigerator cold (at least cool), so I don't open the door. The food in the freezer is already defrosting, so I take out ice cream and eat it with granola, then later eat it again with mixed nuts and more granola.

It's hard to settle. PG&E sends a text: *crew expected onsite by 2:12 PM, 104 houses affected.* It seems our neighborhood and a larger one just beyond us are involuntarily off the grid.

Wind slaps against the house. It is louder than the rain, which is insistent but constrained. The wind chimes in the atrium make bumpy, irregular sounds. I keep thinking the voice I hear from the other room is from the television, but it is only the storm in a conversation of its own.

David Hockey says of La Grande Cour, his old farmhouse/studio in Normandy, "Right now, I need to be somewhere like this. When I signed the lease on Bridlington studio a decade ago, I felt twenty years younger, and the same thing happened here. I feel revitalized. It's given me a new lease on life" (2021, 35).

I have been procrastinating for a while. I have been making other "pictures," to use a Hockney phrase for his work. I've been half-heartedly revising scenes in a novel that half work, and half don't. There is a story within one scene that could be a story itself—I like the idea of story-within-story, but I haven't been able to settle into or figure out if it is worth pursuing or just a distraction. I'm too caught up in the notion of it, not the story itself. The moments I depict are mundane, not meaningful; the characters talk but they don't say anything.

Hockney helps me reconnect to the importance of feeling at home—being able to create a moment of home inside the body, inside the mind, in whatever space is available. It's the awareness of that moment, I'm realizing, that is the thing to settle into. I sense it is what allows creating/artmaking to take place. If I can find home within myself to create, then perhaps I can finally see the space where the story can live. Finding or creating a sense of home within myself, I need that before I settle into my writing.

I love David Hockney because he draws me into his love of making pictures and where and how he works. Yet I know that, for many of us, the space to make art is not (or cannot largely be) physical space but resides primarily inside us.

I live in a house that was big enough when I first got it and is now more space than I need (whatever that means). The space has always been an inspiration to me. I had the fantasy when I moved here that the space would have the feel of an art gallery or 27 rue de Fleurus. I kept the walls white for all the art that I was sure I would hang on them.

Then fifteen minutes into ownership, reality set in. The facts are—there are so many things I've never been able to do with or for this property—and there are many things that have not yet and may never get done here. Just like with writing, what I've accomplished is more limited than I hoped for and bounded by many realities.

And yet, when I open the front door and step in or I sit in a chair and look out—when I watch the light move across the atrium and into the living spaces, the gallery is here. In my mind, there's a place where art lives.

The willingness to put aside all that isn't—or that needs space and time—the willingness to sit in the dark (or partial dark) and let the world outside do its thing, while inside with words and images, with my hand and within my mind, I do mine—that's the reminder that reading David Hockney has offered me.

The rainwater is rising in the side yard. We cleared it out, raked away vines and leaves, so the water would have direct access to a drain, but the rain is too intense. The water is standing, not draining. The wind is quieter, less persistent, still distressing.

The moment is what it is.

David Hockney says, "The place is perfect for me right now. I'm less interested in what other people are doing. I'm just interested in my new work. . ." (2021, 36).

There may be a time when I leave this home or make another somewhere else. It might be a choice or the impact of reality or simply what seems right at the time. This white box of glass and wood I live in is right now available to me, but so is the space inside me. My home, real or imagined, physical or felt, supports me.

The electricity will stay off for another twenty-four hours. Late in the evening, I'll put a flashlight on my shoulder and will pull *Spring Will Not Be Cancelled* close to my face to see the page. David Hockney will say, "If you ask me where I live, I'd always say it's wherever I happen to be," and I'll keep reading (2021, 54).

I found my way home to writing when, like Hockney, I took out a new lease. For me, it was not for land or physical space; it was to try to work with new materials in a new way. It was, as Hockney says, to be less interested in what others were doing and more interested in, more aware of, my work. It was the willingness, not just to be working, but to be engaged. This shift did not actually turn me away from others; it reminded me to be even more curious about how and why they create, and it offered me a place within myself where mostly I could comfortably work. "Mostly" feels important to note. It tells me I don't require surety but is something I can return to again and again.

The image of home I made for *Ten Not-so-Tangible Tools for Writers* was a simple flap in the shape of a house—you could pull it open and step inside, space already there for you.

Writing is being at home.

Be at home in your writing. Feel at home. Be in your home.

Being at home is being comfortable when you write. It allows you to relax into, walk with, own what you have to say. Feeling at home allows you to feel right with, secure in, a belonging to what you have to say. Being in your home means you have a place to go to write. It may be the place where you work or live or a place that you travel to in your mind--but you can step into that place. You can return to it again and again. A room of one's own is important, but to really write, we need to be at home.

Writing arises from solid earth. Home is feeling grounded, connected and calm. Home is really a place—a secure place, a place to take risks, a place to rest or let down. Home base, touchstone, secure attachment are all aspects of home. Home is the place—psychological or physical—where our writing can begin, develop and end. Home provides foundation. Home provides structure. When we are not at home, we wander with our feet and in our hearts and heads. At home, we don't roam. We sit attentively in our chairs and write.

Box 5: Vantage Point/Perspective

Dementia Moment

In the beginning is an image: My father, in some weird mustard-colored shorts and his proverbial white T-shirt, throws a football to a group of neighborhood boys. I stand on the edge of the yard looking into the game—anxious to get in. Not until I pursue the image do details, then a story, emerge.

Between 6930 and 6933 Hubbard Drive was lawn—a field just big enough for touch football games. When I was very young—something like six or seven—I wanted to play with the boys. My brother, the three boys who lived next door, and assorted other boys would gather in the yard—select teams, construct pass plays, wing the football down field, and touch-tackle each other. Often my father, in beige or yellow shorts and a polyester white V-neck T-shirt would come outside to play quarterback for one side or the other. His pants sagged (long before anyone thought of it as urban fashion). He just forgot or was too lazy to put on his belt. So, holding up his shorts with one hand and throwing a spiral with the other, he'd mastermind the game. "I want to play," I said from the strip of yard that slanted uphill—out of the way of hurling bodies but close enough so I could be heard. The boys—my age or a bit older or younger—said no. My father said yes. If the boys wanted him to play, they had to let me join too.

Okay, if they had to.

Reluctantly, the defensive team figured out how to use me. Since I was the smallest child there, I could get low, move stealthily among the bodies, and grab my father at the knees. Once attached, I would hang on for dear life until I brought him down.

I knew the boys didn't want to play with me—and so after a time, I gave up the thrill of pushing myself hard, physically competing with them, being part of the game.

As always, there is a cost to acquiescence. But, for that moment, I knew my father had stood up for me.

I stand up for him now.

*   *   *

I'm with my father in his room at WindChime, a dementia care facility—and, as is my custom when I visit him, I have him stand at the sink in his bathroom, brush his teeth, and use Listerine even though it's midday. If I don't, he'll never take care of his few remaining teeth. He can't wear, let alone manage, dentures anymore. He took them out one day when he was working outside in the yard. Months later we found them misshapen and cracked sitting under a bush.

My cell phone rings, and I go to pick up—it is my brother, who is visiting my aunt in Ashland, Kentucky; it's January 8—our mother's birthday. My brother will visit our mother's grave—something my father has also done on or near this date for years until now. The phone call, like all communications to or visits with my father these days, has multiple layers of meaning. That my father will not think of our mother today or be aware of her birthday or death is an unspoken token of the moment. For my father, the image of Kentucky—my mother's birthplace and his—is what looms large. In some vague way, he senses the "homeplace," but the image sits somewhere between real and unattainable. The phone call activates his desire to see it, that energizes and disorients him at the same time, so much of the experience his life is made up of now.

"Are you still in Lexington?" he asks me as I hand him the phone.

He does not know where he lives. He has been at WindChime, in Northern California, almost five months. My father lived fifty years in Dayton, Ohio, until he came to stay with me in San Rafael a little more than a year ago. This is his first chance to speak to my mother's sister since I moved him into full-time dementia care. Connecting to someone he has had a vital relationship with is still, for now, a lifeline for him. My aunt is the remaining sibling in her family (her two brothers and three sisters are dead) as is my father in his (his three brothers and two sisters are dead)—so they also hold dual connection—as family and longevity representatives. But once on the phone my father can't manage the conversation. He doesn't make much sense—he can start an idea but can't follow it all the way through.

"We got back last night but then all hell broke loose," he says, "I've got nose trouble and can't find my fandango." And then he really starts to ramble.

"Shall we say good-bye? Get some coffee," I say to him. He signs off by telling my aunt in eight or ten days he should be free. He makes it sound like he is on a work trip, but I wonder if somewhere deep inside him the truth longed for within that word is there for him.

Before the cell phone is back in my purse, the connection he's enjoyed is gone, and he succumbs fully to the dementia moment.

The "we" he referred could be me or Pam, the woman who has become his constant companion since her move to WindChime just after his. He often thinks he is Pam's caregiver. Now she waits for him in the middle of the room looking at her own lime-green sweater like she has never seen it before. My father turns to her, "What is your name?" he says.

The essence of my father's Alzheimer's (at least for the present) is represented in the sequence here. There is (1) a short but strong connecting to or recognition of what has been core or central in his life, (2) a being in and enjoying everyday activity which, even on a locked floor, is reminiscent of life before—talking to a family member on the phone, reading the newspaper in the living room, sharing meals with others at a dining room table, and (3) a dementia moment, which usurps everything else. It includes the awful not knowing—Pam's name, that his wife is dead, when he last changed his shirt or sweatpants—and a jumbling of time that combines two or more past experiences into one or joins one or more real experiences with fiction (such as when he told me earlier he was traveling all night and so had to rest after lunch. He did just eat lunch—but, of course, he hasn't traveled anywhere).

"How is Becky?" he asks. His insistent tone tells me his image of her is strong. He is asking about his mother who has been dead since the early 1970s. What to say? Join the moment with him? Tell the truth? Change the subject?

*　*　*

To relate to him, I have to step into whatever moment he is living in. Like any image, to really see it, I have to enter it and let it unfold.

The loss of my father to Alzheimer's is also the loss of a chance to solidify the moments of my family—as the past slips away from him, it slips away from us too. We are left to pursue our images as they come to us, filling in gaps as we can or can't imagine.

Okay, if we have to.

In a way, this seems oddly right—our family stories have always been a mix of fact and fiction.

My father is a storyteller—his life and training have led him to that. A former contract negotiator, arbitrator, and trial attorney, he was often driven and restless, a very competitive personality. An early job in the 1950s after University of Kentucky law school was investigator for the

Civil Service Commission, checking the backgrounds of potential employees for the Atomic Energy Commission. His job was to search out communists in the back woods, dry creeks, and coal-stripped mountains of Kentucky. Also schooled on the streets, he grew up in Lexington as "Little Crow," younger brother of Crow, his brother Amos. He's stubborn about everything—my son and I agree after my father puts up a ruckus about changing his pullover before he goes to lunch or that he put on a pair of shoes that actually fit his feet. Mention a shower—oh my lord, absolute refusal.

What I realize is that my father's personality and training combined to extend the truth—to be hyperbolic—to create a dramatic rendering of a moment or memory. In the 1930s, my father's father left his family, a combination of alcoholism and shame at not being able to find work in the Depression, or infidelity, or all three. So, image—and the strong presence of an older brother—prompted my father from an early age: Poor boy would exceed expectations and make good. It propelled him forward—to graduate high school (something none of his brothers did), determine his way through law school, via the GI Bill, and work at a local grocery store, build a reputable life.

As family members, we used to joke he told and retold stories from his childhood or travels so many times in so many different ways that he no longer knew which version was the truth. But he was true to the moment in which he was telling the story—even if the details or events themselves changed to get at that truth. Was he telling fictional truth? Truthful fiction?

Now dementia places him in an ever-changing moment and he lives there. And that is the truth I now live in too.

*   *   *

The image was clear. The patch of green grass between ours and the neighbor's home. When I stepped into the moment it offered details and the story emerged. Did it happen? I think so. Are the details accurate? They feel right. The story true? My sense of it is true.

More images—My brother's rust-colored 1968 Oldsmobile Cutlass sitting on the slanted driveway humming, the gearshift so tall, I felt I had to reach up for it to drive.

A white 1964 Plymouth station wagon. I sit in the very back—beyond the two rows of red bench seats—to finally get away from everyone and read.

The stupid handmade wood trailer my father built and painted white then backed into a utility pole—his anger at us for not warning him.

The family not talking about the Vietnam War at the dinner table.

White concrete and my father in a dark suit in the hot sun being handed an award for his efforts to build a new YMCA swimming pool.

I try to remember what happened in our family—and what I recall are details and images, moments not memories. Maybe we have always had a family dementia—simultaneously forgetting and remembering—and now my father is just manifesting it, though Becky, his mother, had it long ago. It was just called hardening of the arteries then.

I have a photograph of a stairwell—iron railings and a set of concrete steps—taken by an artist friend many years ago. The image depicts the moment where, in shadow, looking down, the railings on each side of the stairs seems to meet. Of course, the connection is not possible. I've been on that stairwell many times and I know there is a gap, the width of a concrete stair—at least three, maybe four feet—between the two railings. But image joins them, and I believe what I see. The image convinces me.

My heritage and the links to all I am are somewhere in my family images. My father's legacy is the lore that bridges the gaps, and I incorporate it into my being. If I see myself shaped by images as much as experience, what does that mean?

We paint Valentine cards at WindChime. We gather around several tables to work. Vicki is easy; we give her a card, a plastic cup of blue paint, the color of deep ocean water, and she gets to work—dot, dot, dot, across the page. She fills the card with blue dots and then, inexplicably, she balances the blue with valentine red dots also across the expanse of the card. The effect is visually striking—the image, a code indecipherable but engaging. She does not know why she paints dots or what they say or mean, but she steadily moves forward until, for her, the card is done. Others need help. May uses the same blue color as Vicki and with a brush, she writes "love to Mom and Pop" and puts the card aside. I don't know if she is signing the card—is she the Mom of Mom and Pop or she is writing to Mom and Pop? I ask her if she'd like to place something on the front—a heart perhaps for Valentine's Day? She cries. "It's stupid," she says, "to create a valentine for two people who are dead. Everyone is gone." She begins to list the names. I wait, not sure what to say. I tell her my father is the only one still alive from his generation in his family, and we like to say his orneriness is what has gotten him this far. She laughs. You never know about transitions—where the conversation will go next. "He's a smart boy," she says. "I've seen him in action before." Then she smiles. The sadness has passed. I make a red heart for her and then smudge it with the ocean blue paint and a spot of purple to give it dimension and depth.

"Let's do modern art," I say. "What do you think?"

"Fine, just fine," she says. All she wants is a pen. "Love to all," she writes at the bottom of the card.

For my father, life occurs in the immediate moment. My success in dealing with him is linked to how well I can register the moment and respond to it. When I follow his image or moment—as he sees it or describes it—I can still genuinely engage with him, know him, be with him.

He sits at the table with Pam. I ask him if he wants to paint. I hand him some Q-tips and a blank card. His painting is writing sayings inside and outside the card. Every time he stops, I tell him—make another. He does this until he gets tired. The cards say (all in valentine red paint):

- Love is in the glow of heart.

- Love is here. All you have to do is give it away.

- Love is always found—if your eye is pointed right.

- Love is always found first. If the heart sings, so can U.

He understands the essence of what we are doing—he adds red hearts and cupid arrows to the love messages—then he asks, "Where's the boy?"

"Which boy?" I say—never sure if he means my brother or my son or someone else.

"Your boy."

"Back at school," I say.

"You mean in California?" The way he says it lets me know that for him California is an image—not a place, not where he lives.

"Yes," I say then wait for the next moment to begin.

*　*　*　*

Around 2011–2012, I stopped making work in text and image. I don't say "quit" because stopped is the more accurate word. I had to make some choices about how I was going to use my time as a writer/artist with my faculty/administrator commitments. I was ready to return to writing—and honestly did not have time to keep pursuing both. I wasn't fed up or unwilling to make the work. I wanted to write. I decided to give myself all the way to my writing and see what happened—and I wanted to continue to explore how I could develop a visual sensibility, if not actually visual images, in my work.

Memory boxes in words was one way to do that, and I think of "Dementia Moment" as helping to pioneer the work. In them, I wanted to see a memory as accurately as possible, focusing on the details that framed it, boxed it in. I wanted to visualize my experience and write to capture the details of what I see as accurately as I could. I also defined, defined, defined, as a way of understanding the words I used and how they related to the details I documented. The more I learn about what the work (as well as the words) mean, the more I feel I can write to them clearly and relationally.

I wanted "Dementia Moment" to be visually driven. I was also interested in the dailiness of offering, the sensibility of service imbued in the interactions my father and I had with each other and within the facility. What was offered and how? It was a question for me, not an agenda. I looked for what the writing process would offer me—and for what I could offer to it—and I began to write.

One of the things I've learned over the years is that, for me, writing works best when two things are always in play—(1) when there is a relationship alive in the work—materially or via the medium—and (2) I am asking a question that requires me to consider perspective and form, how I am positioning myself in the work and how it is structured. Pursuing these things keeps me learning, something I always want to do in artmaking, and helps me to feel I am making something new, rather than repetitive, a reason to stay with it. I hope it also sustains my relationship with the reader, that they feel connected and curious and get to learn too.

In "Dementia Moment," I wanted the center of attention to be my father. I wanted you to see him and experience him, even though I was using first person. He could not speak for himself any longer in a way that would allow him to tell you how he wanted you to see him, so I needed to evoke him as he was. I wanted to do that visually, not emotionally. I wanted the visual sense of him to be like facts. I also focused on what he said, his actions, events. I did not want to separate him from his Alzheimer's. I did not want it to be unseen. It can't be known if we don't see it. At the time I wrote the piece, my father had lived in a facility for just a few months. At first, he lived with me, but after ten months—with help from experts—I realized everyday life lived in everyday ways was more, much more, than he could handle, and we needed to contain him. We did so by boxing him in a locked floor where he could walk from his room to the kitchen or the living room, bathroom, or another person's bedroom on the floor and nowhere else without someone taking him. I wanted to use that vantage point to make his Alzheimer's visible.

For me, this chapter contains all the boxes—possibility, practice, point of view, play and peace. For example, I bring together practice and point of view in how I depict my father and possibility and play through how I write about image and dementia. Peace—being at home—permeates the piece. Although it broke my heart to place my father in a memory-care facility, he was at home there. On the third floor of WindChime, he could read the newspaper, the same one over and over, forget where his room was and just take a nap in someone else's, or wave his hand in delight when his "buddy," my son (he was sure they were buddies, never mind his name) came to visit. He could just settle in. That settling in—for him, physical and emotional, for me, into the images, gave me a "home" from which to let this piece emerge.

I thought I would write more about that time and my father, but I haven't and I'm not sure I will. I've shown what I wanted to. Originally, I wrote a sentence saying I can't really see who my father is in his fullness anymore, just who he became in that long slow process of Alzheimer's dismantling all he had been. But there is this:

Image #1: In 2008, a year before my father comes to live with me, he flies in for a visit. For the first time, I've told him not to rent a car. That means while I am working, he is hanging out. It's early afternoon, just after lunch, and he is stretched out on the couch, lying on his left side, pillow, as always, since hip surgery, between his knees. The TV hums, and Johnny, our sweet black cat, rests comfortably on his hip. They don't move; they are resting and at peace. Later, he'll say what a good nap he had.

Image #2: I call my father and ask him how his flight home was. He tells me everything was fine until he got to LA and had a huge, infuriating, layover. No one would help him. He was there for hours. The distress in his voice is real. I drove my father to SFO the day before and made sure his direct flight was all set before I left for home. He was nowhere near Los Angeles the previous day. I listen, my body aware of how crazy what he is saying is. I want to ask questions, tell him it didn't happen, to offer facts—but I realize, for him, this imagined memory is real—and fear for him and for us sets in.

The images are distinct—and I start to say because they are so different I can't make a box of them. But I can open a box and place them in it. I feel my responsibility as a writer is to let them, like my father at WindChime, settle in, and, if others arise, to place them too, no agenda beyond that.

Resources

Definitions

Fervor: https://www.etymonline.com/search?q=fervor
Dance: https://www.merriam-webster.com/dictionary/dance
Osmosis: https://dictionary.cambridge.org/us/dictionary/english/osmosis
Being: https://www.merriam-webster.com/dictionary/being
Play: https://www.etymonline.com/search?q=play

Books and Websites

Bogart, Anne, (2007), *And Then, You Act*. Routledge, 53–54:
"Attention is about going beyond self-interest but at the same time remaining intensely in tune and responsive within."
Fuentes, Carlos, (2005), *The Diary of Frida Kahlo: An Intimate Self Portrait*, Abrams.
Grahn, Judy, (2012), *A Simple Revolution*, Aunt Lute Books.
See also https://judygrahn.org and Kelly, Catherine. "The Women's Press Collective, 1969–77," https://www.chicagoreview.org/the-womens-press-collective-1969-1977/.
King, Alonzo: https://linesballet.org/lines-ballet-mission-and-purpose/alonzo-king/
"Brief but Spectacular," Alonzo King on PBS, https://www.youtube.com/watch?v=Lwh8Ugz_f8M&list=PLvkDqCCfq21HgA6H8M7U51Sg5UAa2aARt&index=1.
Alonzo King: Making of "Scheherazade" with Alonzo King LINES Ballet, 2012, https://www.youtube.com/watch?v=Km5fClRBimM.
Kraft, Richard, (2021), *It Is What It Is: All the Cards Issued to Donald Trump*, Volumes 1–5 (January 2017–January 2021), Siglio.
Laurence, Madeline, (2008), *Correspondence: Pablo Picasso and Gertrude Stein*, Seagull Books.
Levitin, Daniel, (2013), "What Makes a Musician?" *This is Your Brain on Music*, Plume/Penguin.
Marclay, Christian and Steve Beresford, (2021), *Call and Response*. Siglio Press.
Nottage, Lynn, (2005), *Intimate Apparel*, Dramatist's Play Service.
Snyder, Gary. "A Letter to M.A., Who Lives Far Away," *American Scholar*, Summer 2009: 55

Reading: https://voca.arizona.edu/track/id/57144.

Yang, Gene Luen, (2007), *American Born Chinese*, First Second.

Reflection and Exercises

If I were to make a postcard of this chapter, I'd draw a box, of course. I'd leave the lid open so you could see all the space it has and all it could hold. I'd write, "What's in your box? Will you let us see inside it?" I'd wonder if you'd fill it, pack it carefully, wrap what's inside. For the stamp, I'd have a box with a closed lid. On it or around the rim of the lid (this might be more interesting visually), I'd cut out words from the images/memories I've included in this chapter, and I'd borrow from the USA postal service and write ~~forever~~ in the script that they use, since what we remember shifts and changes as we do.

What is your postcard in response to this chapter? I hope you'll imagine it or make it. For me, each of the boxes in this chapter suggests a tool (and choices you can probe). I hope you'll reflect on them and in your journal respond to these questions:

Possibility—What is your experience of other arts? How do they offer you possibility for your work? Or what are sources of possibility for you? Which might you try out?

Practice: Why do you practice? As repetition and/or to further develop patterns or options for your work? Or to explore and discover? Or?

For a week, log your practice, track your habits. Reflect on what you learn.

What are ways of knowing your work? Like Judy Grahn, try to articulate your writing. What happens when you try? Focus on what matters to you—what do you care about and value? What or who influences your work?

Then review a piece or two of your writing. How do your responses here match what you articulate? What is the same or what's different or missing? What could you be more curious about or probe more to meet your hopes for it?

Please do this process gently. You are just in a conversation with yourself, not trying to get it right or see how little you know or how the work doesn't meet your expectations. What we want to reach for and what we can create (because of our knowledge, insight, capacity, time, skill sets and more) are in dialogue with each other. How you talk to yourself in that relationship is important. Please be kind and careful—

and give yourself room to keep trying, keep learning—and feel good/confident (congratulate yourself) when you can both speak about the work and create what you want to. That is a lot to feel proud of.

Play: Do you play to see what happens and/or play to see what emerges? Or both? How do you play with mediums, forms, meanings? Why?

Again, for a week, try to build play into your practice sessions. Take 10 minutes or so at the start of a session and play with an idea or with an approach (for example, playing with being as visual as you can or focusing on including taste or touch or sound into the work), or a different point of view or vantage point. Play with your tone or attitude. Maybe write as if you are someone else. Play can make us aware of aspects of ourselves or skill sets or insights we didn't know we had. Why not use play to get to know yourself differently—and see where it leads?

Place/Peace: When do you feel at home in your work? How does that feeling help you with writing? When you don't feel at home in your writing, how could you draw from your feeling of being at home to help you make your work? What might help you do that?

Here I suggest making an image: What does the feeling of being at home in your work look like to you? Or draw yourself at home—and reflect on how you create that feeling or want to.

You can draw, paint, collage the image—or you can visualize it and write it focusing on capturing what you see as much as you can. Perhaps use it as a talisman, a reference point, for when getting into or staying with writing when you are restless or it is hard.

Vantage Point/Perspective: How do you recognize vantage point in your writing? How do you use it to shape your writing?

Review some work and note how you locate yourself or your narrator in it. How close in the moments or action are you? How much distance do you create between the character and their actions and where you or your narrators tell the story? How does your vantage point align with your values—and your hopes for the work?

Pick one piece you'd like to do more with—and shift the vantage point and the point of view. Retell the story. Compare it to the other version. Reflect on the process and what you learn. Do you want to shift your vantage point or develop more dexterity in your work?

In this chapter, I've wanted to highlight the value and benefit of possibility, practice, play, place/peace, and vantage point/perspective. I also wanted to show you the interplay between and among them in my writing—and how being conscious of that interplay can benefit your writing. As you read this book, I hope you'll reflect on these questions: What relationships, intersections, and the connections among them can provoke your most realized work? What choices do they offer you and what do you feel ready to pursue?

Also important, how would you define each of the boxes in this chapter ? How do you relate to and use them? Or what is missing for you from the boxes I provide? What would you draw on to create? List that and articulate it.

Where your ideas or hopes for you work differ from mine, please note that. I believe those can be valuable tools for you. I hope you'll name them—and give them form so you can refer to them whenever you need them.

4 A CIRCUITOUS BUT SUSTAINABLE WRITER'S LIFE

Writing is Word and Image Working Together

Writing is individual words and words in relationship to words. Each word matters, counts, belongs. Image heightens the meaning and enhances the effect of words. When word joins image, and image joins word, writing has more dimension and depth.

I am using the word *image* here in two ways—one, to mean images that words create and, two, to mean images that are visually constructed. Creating image with words and constructing visual images can benefit writers. First, images created with words appeal to the senses and suggest detail, symbols, and pictures. Images depicted in words give us more than concepts and feelings. They allow for the sensate and provide for the sensual. Working together, word and image evoke *and* articulate experience.

Second, word and visual image can also work together—by allowing a visual object to work with the words on the page. Writers can benefit from understanding and working with core images. Creating and exploring images can help us to understand the symbols, experiences, feelings, and issues that are beyond words in our work. Also, visual images can be like talismans—serving as guides or helpers as we write. They can allow us to seek and explore personal connections. They can also reassure and encourage us to write more deeply.

Ten Not-So-Tangible Tools for Writers, mixed media, 2001

Years ago, I worked with a graduate student and noticed the frequent use of a wrapped female figure in her paintings. I asked about the image and why it was important to her work. She wasn't sure. I asked her if she'd be willing to reflect on the image and write about it—and she did. She wrote about her paintings, remembered moments in her life, and wrote about them. Over time, the more she got to know the image, it unwrapped. A new female image emerged. The figure was visible; she might bend or share the canvas with text, or glass or stone might shape her figure, and she wasn't wrapped. The wrapped image was beautiful, often haunting but beautiful. The figure didn't have to change, but once the artist got to know the image, she didn't want to be bound by it. She wanted to change it, or she changed and so changed the image. She began to see her images differently and the different seeing led to different images. This student made visual art, but the learning working with her gave me extends to writers: When we are willing to see and see into our images, we learn from them and then can decide if we want to continue to make them or shift, alter, or re-direct our work. We add to our choices and how we can work with them.

In *Create Dangerously: The Immigrant Artist at Work*, Edwidge Danticat says, "All artists, writers among them, have several stories—one might call them creation myths—that haunt and obsess them" (2011, 5). Important to her is the grievous story of Marcel Numa and Luis Drouin, *Jeune Haiti* members, who were captured and put to death by Francois Duvalier's government in 1964. I understand her to be saying a creation myth stays with us because it arises from something specific and very real. Danticat invites us to be aware of the something, to let it live within us, even when it is difficult or painful to take in. It is there for us to see, to recognize, and we decide when we'll get to know it and how it will live in our writing.

The stories I tell in this book have taught me that our very real lives influence and have an impact on our writing. What happens in our cultures and lives also happens to us as artists and so happens to our writing. The stories I tell here share some of the realities that shape my life as artist but, of course, there are lots of other realities and other stories that only briefly appear or aren't here at all. There are also many things happening right now so I may be living them rather than writing them. All my experience influences and shapes me, as I believe, does yours. Image, I've tried to show here, is a way into what we see and what is within our experience; great, if we can see it all—see ourselves fully, see the context that shapes our experience, but whatever we can see leads us to choices for writing. Seeing leads to what, right now, we are able to say.

I've also seen that how we read our work influences our capacity to create and sustain it. An MFA student and I met to talk about her novel in progress. I placed questions in the text as I was reading and in notes at the end, asking things like if she wanted me to believe what the character said or if, I should doubt her perspective. I asked if she wanted me, as reader, to be part of the character's experience, close in with her, or looking at it from a distance, and why one character important to the story wasn't more visible. I asked how the story might shift if we met her in section one, rather than section three. I also asked questions about use of verbs, why the tone shifted in the final section, what some words meant to her and why she chose them, and how plot-driven she wanted the work to be, among other things.

She asked me how did I know to ask my questions—or to ask questions at all? Great question—How did I acquire that skill? I shared how, over time, I learned to read as writer and reader. As writer, I try to feel into what the writer is reaching for and to read from that perspective: What are the writer's choices and how are they implementing them? What are the possibilities and limits of the writer's perspective and hopes for the piece?

As a reader, I read, first, as myself, sharing my experience of what happens when I read (from what confuses me to what delights me and why), and, second, I try to read as someone unaware of the book, trying to decide if I'll stay with it (press, publisher, agent, person at the bookstore or airport market). I take my reading experience and selectively note it. I focus on questions, not on advice, because I think questions lead to options—and to be able to rely on ourselves when we need to make choices about them, we need to know the options and/or be ready to create them ourselves. A writing community is very important but, I feel, so is being able to coach yourself. I want my response to be relational, one that says to the writer here is how I read your work. I want to invite the writer to ask more about my reading experience and how I read the work. I hope my reading also suggests or shares with them additional ways they can read their work. If we just take in what a reader tells us and don't ask how they arrived at their reading, we may give away choices that will help us revise. I've acknowledged it is hard to stay with a writing project if you don't feel you have the skills to take it all the way through the process. Being writer and reader of your work can support you and the work, so can a toolbox.

FIGURE 7 *Ten Not-So-Tangible Tools for Writers Toolbox*, 2001.
Wood box, found objects, handmade papers, oil pastels, puzzle pieces, watercolor paper

The toolbox I created for *Ten-Not-So Tangible for Writers* was dark wood with a rounded, half-dome lid. I bought it at Pier One. I wanted writers to be able to open it and find what they needed to commit (or re-commit) to and enjoy their writing. The box had a muted gold clasp and handle, so it could be carried anywhere. Inside, there was a cinnamon container, made in Vietnam, filled with small objects to inspire the work, a hand-made bag of puzzle pieces to remind writers they could play with how they constructed their writing, an alter crafted out of 300-lb watercolor paper and scraps of wrapping paper, the ten tools printed on handmade paper and on paper strips placed in a small blue container on the writing table so writers could pull them out like fortunes or for support. When I look at the photo now, I note the two figures, sitting together, like they are waving at writers, calling them into the space. Blues and greens are prevalent, colors of peacefulness and inspiration, growth and fertility. I debated this photo or another in which the view of the figures was closer in, but I didn't want to overemphasize the welcoming characters—they are part of the process, but the whole box, all that it holds, everything we need to make our work—that's what I wanted the box to offer. I hope you'll imagine your toolbox and all it holds.

Curiosity and A Final Exercise

Note: You'll need your notebook for this section.

At the end of each chapter, I asked you to reflect on items presented in the chapter and tools I use or choices I've made and to test out or play with anything that interested you. I also invited you to use my writing as a catalyst to help you list what you care about in your writing or tools you might like to create for yourself. I provided some exercises and encouraged you to see what they might yield you.

Now, I'd like to ask you to review it all—read over/review everything you've created. Read over the body of work you have. Read as you (writer); read as your reader (observer). What stands out for you? Is there recurring image or a quiet creation myth influencing your writing? When/how do you notice aspects of your process or decisions about craft or structure? What choices have you made and what do they tell you about your writing?

Then, list your choices; note the tools you use or want to develop. What are you learning that you want to keep pursuing? Reflect on these things and ask yourself—what's missing? I have always been curious how writing/artwork is made; now, I also focus on why. After writing this book, I realize curiosity is a tool. *Curiosity* feels direct and playful; like it can actively steer us through our writing. it can drive the directions of our writing.

Curiosity permeates all aspects of my work. For example, recently, I started out curious about Chapter Three. I had a story I wanted to include in it. I wrote a draft, and it felt whiny; I didn't want that, so I re-worked it. The second draft felt pompous, bloated; I definitely didn't want that. I couldn't clearly see the core of the experience and how it related to the story. I started out inquisitive, but I couldn't get the moment right, I couldn't clearly see the experience, so I shifted my attention to another part of the chapter. I noted more and more things that needed to be edited or removed or were not working; I was no longer curious, just overwhelmed and very aware I had a lot of work to do. I took a break and started again—re-focusing. I remembered I didn't have to re-write the whole chapter that day. Most important, I told myself, stay interested, stay curious so I could be in dialogue with the chapter. I did, and I not only made progress on the chapter, but I discovered why the story I wanted to include didn't work: It didn't fit. It belonged in another chapter. Staying curious about what fit and what didn't also helped me revise two other sections of the chapter.

Another example: When I wrote about the student's wrapped image, I had a clear sense and my experience of it, but it has been more than twenty years since I've seen the image. I logged into the library and brought up the student's dissertation. I went to her artist website to look at her current work and archive—I wanted to research—to see again—what I thought I knew to test the accuracy of my memory. I was curious what I'd find—and I did rewrite several sentences, adding the detail about her placing text in her paintings. The research reminded me it was very important to her work. She always wrote about her paintings, but as her image-making became freer, she also felt more free to bring language, which she cares a lot about, into the work too.

I hope you'll continue to notice how writers make choices and use tools and develop them as your own. Keep a notebook close by when you read and write. When you read, note when you are learning something from a writer. But mostly stay curious and learn from yourself. Like Annie B. Parson, chart, note, or draw. You can probe what you note or not but do record what stands out for you. Keeping notes, recording details, documenting gives you something you can return to again and again. If or when you are ready, you can inquire into, reflect on, and/or expand on what's there—and do more with it.

Your Writing Tools: Next Steps

Once you name tools or understandings that feel right to you and you know you want to work with them, please do this:

- List and describe them as I have done with *Ten Not-So-Tangible Tools for Writers*. If you use some of my tools, revise or update them for your needs.

- If a text/image approach interests you, make your tool. Get a blank card, write, draw, paint, collage or make an object-tool (that could be fun). Find a box or make one and place your tools in it. Use them for guidance, as resources, and inspiration.

- Use your tools to write a new piece. Refer to or reflect on them before you write, but once you start writing, just write. Put them away while you write.

- Once you have a draft, return to your tools. Reflect on how they guide you, how they influence the work. Focus on the ways you are using them. Don't focus on how you didn't live up to them or how you failed. Try another draft. Stay curious about the tools and your piece—and just write. Once you have a new draft, reflect again. Note which tools are easy for you to use, that you feel aligned with. Keep working with them. The others? Continue to be curious—probe them as you can. Let the tools continue to develop as your work does. Let their influence on you develop as the work does.

Final Postcard

Imagine a story of staying with writing. Look into the future—six months, a year, five years—and create a scene or a moment in time in which you will have to choose staying with it or not. Write that scene/moment, read it, and review the images within it. Pick one image, make it, and place it on one side of the card.

Then decide who you'll send the card to: Are you writing to yourself or someone you want to make aware of this moment? Reflecting on the image you've made, reduce the text to what needs to be said or write a message the moment invites you to share. Then make your stamp—a stamp of commitment to staying with it?

Send the card or keep it. Either way what you say will stay with you. Review it or remember it whenever you need to. You might keep it in your toolbox or take a photo of it and create a Toolbox folder and place it there.

Or—in your notebook, create a tool: *Writing is Staying With It*. What do you see when you say that? Create the image. Then create the text. Place it where you can access it whenever you need it.

From Loss to Lease

As David Hockney said, it is okay to take out a new lease. You can move to a new place or find a new one within yourself to write, start again, reconnect with your writing (even be playful), and settle in.

In 2021, I made a podcast, *Lost-proof*, for *Artifact*, sponsored by our MFA. In the series, each artist got an object, a sky-blue Pentalic Traveler Journal, and then made something out of or in response to it. I associated

FIGURE 8 *Loss-~~proof~~*, Postcard, "6 x 8", 2021.

Mixed Media paper, stencils, flowers oil pastels, printed dictionary definitions

the word *travel* with trip—and, not being able to travel because of the pandemic, I took a walk as a trip and recorded it in my journal. Then, as you can probably guess, I made a postcard.

The day of my trip I learned that 3,000,000 people world-wide had died of Covid. I held that steep loss and the number in my mind as I walked. I also noticed many new For Lease signs, also signs of loss, as I walked by several local shopping centers; so many businesses consolidating, moving, abruptly shutting down. I thought of the phrase *a new lease on life*. I wondered—What would it mean to take out a new lease in a time of loss?

One side of the postcard plays with the idea of loss sending a message "For Lease," sharing a stamp with a figure wearing a thin banner of loss-~~proof~~. The other (depicted here) "From Loss," shares definitions of lease that include to let or let go. I placed, on a re-offered figure from an earlier postcard, white flower petals and California poppies, which are with us only a few weeks in the spring, Loss and life, a lease between.

The postcard reminds me loss is not failure; it's loss. That is something I shared in Chapter 1. I know loss and failure (or the feeling of failure) can shutter our work—and what can be found may not be readily available or clear. Our lease between? Our tools, choices, curiosity, awareness. With them we can let go of what keeps us from or limits our work. They let us stay with our writing.

*   *   *

Writing is a relationship that, among other things, invites us to make use of our tools and understandings, our choices and capacities to act on them, and the possibilities all arts and artists offer us. Being a writer is a relationship with all we have been exposed to. I am reflecting on the lives and writing/art of those I have been exposed to—and the many ways they have brought their work to the world—through commercial publishing houses and crow-funded publishers, university, feminist, independent, and small presses or presses they founded, self-publishing or by reading their work in bars, at universities, on streets or stages in protest or celebration. They have published via mimeograph, broadsheet, hand-made books, text-image objects, hardback, paperback, e-book, print on demand, and audiobook. They have developed or directed their own arts organizations or degree programs, been interviewed for podcasts, television and film or by the press or featured on PBS. They have received an honorary doctorate or had lifetime achievement awards named for them, received grants, cultivated donors, built their careers through collaboration and fundraising, activism and travel, via Instagram, Facebook, and Substack—and with care and support from communities, friends, family, and other artists.

There are so many ways to bring your writing/art to an audience. You can be the writer/artist you want to be. I hope you'll pursue how all book art, zines, magazines, journals, or books (also e-books and audiobooks) you like are printed or published—and how they connect with an audience.

Begin, however, in finding your work and leasing yourself to it—and then let others and their publications lead you from here. Find your work and make it—then make something of it. All the writers/artists I've mentioned in this book and so many more have and continue to be teachers/mentors to me. I've wanted to show how I have been mentored, sometimes by artists, sometimes by their work (and you can be too)—and offer this book as a relationship that supports you and, as my student asked me to, inspire you: Stay with it. Stay with it. Stay with your writing.

Resources

Lost-~~proof~~, Artifact podcast, Mission at Tenth, 05/05/21, https://www.missionattenth.com/artifact/lost-proof

Cotter, Lucy, editor, (2024), *Reclaiming Artistic Research*, Expanded Second Edition, Hatje Cantz, 530–31. She speaks of the not knowing artists engage in and how we are trying to "articulate new questions," not find answers in artmaking.

REFERENCES

Alam, Rumaan, (2020), "How Author-Illustrator Maira Kalman begins the Perfect Work Day." Posted by Slate.com, April 13, 2020, https://slate.com/culture/2020/04/maira-kalmans-perfect-work-day.html.

Allen, Pat B., (1995), *Art is a Way of Knowing*, Shambhala.

Barry, Lynda, (2008), *What It Is*, Drawn & Quarterly.

Bogart, Anne, (2007), *And Then, You Act*, Routledge.

Bogart, Anne, (2021), *The Art of Resonance*, Methuen Drama, Bloomsbury Publishing.

Coates, Nigel, (2012), *Narrative Architecture*, John Wiley & Sons.

Coleman, Elliott, (1980), *Four Counties of Youth*, Geryon Press.

Cotter, Lucy, ed., (2024), "Research as Play: Dialogue with Ryan Gander," *Reclaiming Artist Research*, Expanded Section Edition, Berlin: Hatje Cantz.

Danticat, Edwidge, (2010), *Create Dangerously: The Immigrant Artist at Work*, Princeton University Press.

Edwards, Betty, (1979), *Drawing on the Right Side of the Brain*, Penguin Putnam.

Finlay, Victoria, (2004), *Color: A Natural History of the Palette*, Random House Trade Paperback.

Frank, Joan, (2008), *Cherry Hill: A Childhood Reimagined*, The Monacelli Press.

Grahn, Judy, (2008), *love belongs to those who do the feeling: New and Selected Poems*, Red Hen Press.

Hartmann, Elizabeth, (2016), "The Most Modern 18th-Century Room You've Ever Seen." Posted by the Wall Street Journal, Feb. 25, 2016, https://www.wsj.com/articles/the-most-modern-18th-century-room-youve-ever-seen-1456423326.

Hockney, David, and Martin Gayford, (2021), *Spring Cannot Be Cancelled: David Hockney in Normandy*, Thames & Hudson.

King, Alonzo, (2011), "Art Thought," *Mission at Tenth Inter-arts Journal*, 2, 85–88, CIIS, Interdisciplinary Arts Department.

Krug, Nora, (2023), *Diaries of War: Two Visual Accounts from Ukraine and Russia*, Ten Speed Graphic.

O'Keane, Veronica, (2021), *A Sense of Self: Memory, The Brain and Who We Are*, W.W. Norton & Company.

Parson, Annie-B, (2019), *Drawing the Surface of Dance: A Biography in Charts*, Wesleyan University Press.

Redniss, Lauren, (2015), *Radioactive: Marie & Pierre Curie: A Tale of Love and Fallout*, Dey Street Books.

Schaffner, Ingrid, (2010), "Exaltations/Observations," *Maira Kalman, Various Illuminations of a Crazy World*, 69–71, Institute of Contemporary Arts and DelMonico Books.

Schalansky, Judith, (2020), *Inventory of Losses*, New Directions.

Schalansky, Judith, (2010), *Pocket Atlas of Remote Islands: Fifty Islands I Have Not Visited and Never Will*, Penguin.

Sharpe, Christina, (2023), *Ordinary Notes*, Farrar, Straus & Giroux.

Solnit, Rebecca, (2005), *A Field Guide to Getting Lost*, Penguin Books.

St. Clair, Kassia, (2016), *The Secret Lives of Color*, Penguin Books.

"Understanding Historic Parks and Gardens in Buckinghamshire" (2019), The Buckinghamshire Gardens Trust Research & Recording Project, Bucks Garden Trust Report. https://bucksgardenstrust.org.uk/wp-content/uploads/2019/01/Chilton_House.pdf.